9.00 C 9.5

Rory Osbourne

D0871988

MENTAL IMAGERY

MENTAL IMAGERY

ALAN RICHARDSON

SPRINGER PUBLISHING COMPANY, INC.
NEW YORK

Springer Publishing Company, Inc.
200 Park Avenue South   New York, New York 10003

© Alan Richardson 1969

Library of Congress Catalog Card Number: 70-78913

Printed in Great Britain

To
My Mother and Father

'It is a fascinating study in the psychology of the scientific mind to note the curious fluctuations in its interests from one decade to another . . . At one time much work will be motivated by a particular interest, then another topic comes to the fore; later on another still. By the time that the first topic is focused again it is necessary to modify the treatment of it by the new discoveries made in other fields. This is what has happened concerning the doctrine of the image.'

Downey, 1929, p. 35

CONTENTS

FOREWORD

IT IS the purpose of this book to bring together in one place a representative sample of facts and hypotheses concerning the phenomena of mental imagery. The time seems to be appropriate for such an attempt, and it is hoped that it will serve as a guide to research in this field until a more comprehensive treatment becomes available.

The field covered under the heading of mental imagery is a large one and relevant material spans the entire history of experimental psychology. In 1860 Gustav Fechner (1966) discussed the topic in his book on the *Elements of Psychophysics*. In 1880, at the very beginning of research into the nature of individual differences, Francis Galton carried out a statistical investigation into the varieties of imagery reported by school boys, artists, scientists and statesmen.

From the days of Wilhelm Wundt at Leipzig to the end of Edward Bradford Titchener's time at Cornell University, the image constituted a basic theoretical element in the psychological system of the structuralists, but with the decline of structuralism and the growth of behaviourism in the 1920's, mental imagery began to fade as a serious subject for investigation and completely disappeared as a theoretical construct. Only a few intrepid characters like Emeritus Professor T. H. Pear of Manchester University continued to talk and write about imagery during the great eclipse (Pear, 1927, 1935, 1937; Kerr and Pear, 1931). From the late 1920's till the late 1940's the attention of most academic psychologists in the English speaking world was focused upon other problems, notably upon theoretical issues in the field of learning.

However, from the early 1950's until the present time academic psychology has expanded its range of research enormously, and one of the areas which has shown an extraordinarily vigorous growth is that concerning cognitive processes, of which the activity of imaging is one.

Many theoretical and practical problems have contributed to this revival of interest, and in his article on 'Imagery: the Return of the Ostracized' Robert Holt (1964) provides a vivid account of their nature. In writing of the practical problems of an ergonomic kind, he cites the examples of: 'Radar operators who have to monitor a scope for long periods; long-distance truck drivers in night runs over turnpikes, but also victims of "highway hypnosis"; jet pilots flying straight and level at high altitudes; operators of snowcats and other such vehicles of polar exploration, when surrounded by snow storms—all of these persons have been troubled by the emergence into consciousness of vivid imagery, largely visual but often kinaesthetic or auditory, which they may take momentarily for reality.'

In the situations just described the emergence of imagination imagery is potentially dangerous, and an understanding of the conditions of its occurrence is necessary if it is to be controlled or eliminated. But like most other events, the spontaneous emergence of imagination imagery has a positive as well as a negative side. Imagination imagery has traditionally been associated with acts of creation, particularly during the illumination phase, and it seems reasonable to expect that a more exact study of the part played by mental imagery, of all kinds, in the processes of creation will increase our knowledge of this highly valued activity and its products.

Practical problems of the kind outlined raise theoretical issues, both within psychology and within allied disciplines like neurophysiology. Within psychology, for example, there has been an increase of interest in the place of mental imagery in the general process of cognitive development (e.g. Werner and Kaplan, 1963; Bruner, et al., 1966). Within neurophysiology the reports of imagery that have accompanied stimulation of points on the exposed temporal cortex of epileptic patients have aroused considerable theoretical interest (Penfield and Roberts, 1959). What kind of brain mechanisms mediate the retention and recovery of these strips of vivid quasi-sensory and affective memories?

To get some perspective on the nature of mental imagery and the theoretical, practical and methodological problems that are raised by its existence, a considerable range of literature has been examined; but relevant research and discussion on mental imagery have appeared in a wide variety of languages and in an even wider variety of journals, so that the task of covering it all, with even partial completeness, has been a difficult one. The task is made more difficult by the long time span of more than 100 years and the absence of any systematic reviews of the literature. The effect of these difficulties has been to bias the selection of material in some known and some unknown ways. Most of the literature cited has been published in English; most often this has been the original language of publication but sometimes it has been the result of translation. Writers who have been primarily philosophical, psychopharmacological or neuro-physiological in their interests are very poorly represented, as are psychologists whose accounts have been mainly anecdotal. In addition it will be noted that certain traditional topics, such as the relation of mental imagery to literature or to education, have been almost completely ignored.

What has been deliberately included has been as much empirical material of a behavioural and experiential kind (Richardson, 1965) as relates to the nature of imagery *qua* imagery and as relates to the part played by imagery in such other cognitive processes as perception, remembering and thinking. In addition, a considerable amount of space has been devoted to the consideration of methodological issues, especially the difficult but crucial problem of finding objective neurological, physiological or behavioural indices that parallel subjective reports of mental imagery or in some other way provide checks upon the accuracy or utility of such reports.

The first chapter of this book takes up the problem of defining mental imagery so that all subclasses of imagery would be encompassed. In the four chapters that follow, each major subclass of imagery has been discussed in turn: after imagery and related phenomena, eidetic imagery, memory imagery, and lastly, imagination imagery. The final chapter attempts a brief restatement concerning the two major phenomenal attributes of mental imagery—vividness and controllability—and then goes on to discuss some particular cognitive problems in which the process of imaging is involved.

Acknowledgements are due to many colleagues and friends in Australia and overseas who were kind enough to comment on a first draft of this book. In particular I would like to thank: A. J. Marshall, J. Ross and J. Lumsden from the University of Western Australia; R. R. Brown from the Australian National

University; R. Taft from the University of Melbourne; E. L. Hartley from the City University of New York, and Professor Emeritus T. H. Pear, late of Manchester University. All of them helped by disengaging their minds from other important matters to give their time and thought to some of the problems discussed here. For permission to reproduce the vividness of imagery scale (Appendix A) I am indebted to P. W. Sheehan of New England University. My thanks are also due to Rosemary Gordon of London University who gave permission to reproduce a slightly modified version of her test of visual imagery control (Appendix B).

Chapter *1*

DEFINING MENTAL IMAGERY

ARTISTS and philosophers have usually been particularly sensitive to the fragile and fluctuating boundary between fantasy and reality. The rest of us have muddled through and felt that our personal survival was proof enough that we could make the distinction when it really counted. Our hold on the real world may be precarious but it is also tenacious, and science as a method and as a creed has been enthusiastically espoused because it has made our hold just that much stronger.

The philosophical problem of distinguishing between fantasy and reality partly resolves itself into the search for grounds on which to accept or reject the proposition that true knowledge of reality can be gained through the senses. The problem in just this form goes beyond the competence of the present writer and somewhat beyond the stated purpose of this book. However, the interested reader will find a particularly valuable philosophical analysis by Professor R. J. Hirst who has collaborated with a psychologist and a biologist to write a book on the human senses and perceptions (Wyburn, Pickford and Hirst, 1964).

In the days, not long ago, when experimental psychologists were often physiologists and philosophers as well, a good deal of attention was paid to the empirical task of discovering the conditions under which their subjects distinguished, or failed to distinguish, between images and percepts and how, at a neurophysiological level, a distinction might be made between the processes of imaging and perceiving. When images ceased to be of interest to psychologists this problem was necessarily shelved, and even now with the revival of interest in these problems, no generally accepted solution has been found.

Nevertheless, in outlining a working definition of mental imagery an attempt has been made to distinguish an image from a percept, first, in terms of its subjectively experienced properties and secondly, in terms of its objectively observable antecedents and consequents. This attempt has not been entirely successful; neither the subjective nor the objective criteria are infallible. However, the attempt to indicate some of the limiting conditions, where differentiation appears to break down, does serve to emphasize certain points of similarity and of difference between the nature of images and imaging on the one hand and the nature of percepts and perceiving on the other.

In the past mental imagery has been defined in a variety of ways, but none of them is entirely adequate for our purpose either. For example, Oswald Külpe's (1893) definition of images as 'centrally excited sensations' implies that peripheral stimulation plays no part in the formation of a mental image. Though this is obviously untrue of the common after-image it is probably untrue of other varieties of mental imagery as well. Again, Leuba's (1940) definition of mental images as 'conditioned sensations', though it may apply to spontaneous memory images, is unsatisfactory if applied to imagination images.

Now one difficulty with previous definitions is that they only describe or account for certain limited forms of mental imagery, whereas the definition required here is one that will cover the entire range of mental imagery. As with the definition of most complex concepts the definition of mental imagery requires that we examine all the particular examples that comprise it, before we are likely to understand its meaning. It is hoped that a reading of the chapters on after imagery, eidetic imagery, memory imagery and imagination imagery will help to provide this kind of ostensive definition. Nevertheless, some attempt at a formal definition will be made and each of its parts will serve to highlight the very real difficulty, already noted, of finding absolute criteria for separating the concept of an image from that of a percept.

Mental imagery refers to (1) all those quasi-sensory or quasi-perceptual experiences of which (2) we are self-consciously aware, and which (3) exist for us in the absence of those stimulus conditions that are known to produce their genuine sensory or perceptual counterparts, and which (4) may be expected to have different consequences from their sensory or perceptual counterparts.

By 'quasi-sensory or quasi-perceptual experiences' is meant any concrete re-presentation of sensory, perceptual, affective or other experiential states (e.g. hunger or fatigue). On a first impression there is something paradoxical about the notion of a quasi-affective state. Ribot (1911) observed: 'Some people have a *false* or *abstract* memory for feelings, others a *true* or *concrete* one. In the former the image is scarcely revived, or not at all, in others it is revived in great part, or totally.' When it is revived 'in great part, or totally' it 'consists in the *actual* reproduction of a former state of feeling'. To blush with shame at the memory of an unkind action is an obvious example. The autonomic nervous system is aroused in relation to the complex of thoughts associated with the memory and we say that we feel the same emotion. That is, we apply the same verbal label of 'shame' to the original experience complex and to its reconstruction, though the actual antecedent conditions are different on the two occasions. It may well prove to be the case that a quasi-perceptual experience, in the form of a visual image, involves the reactivation of those neuro-physiological processes of the central nervous system that were activated during the original perceptual experience (see p. 11 of this book, and Zikmund, 1966). Perhaps the main difference between a quasi-sensory or perceptual experience and a quasi-affective experience is that the experienced effects of c.n.s. activity are so much 'quieter' than those of the a.n.s. and for this reason are more difficult to discriminate. To be 'self consciously aware' of these concrete re-presentations means that the individual should be able to report on what he has 'seen', 'heard', 'touched' 'tasted', 'smelled', or 'felt'. For experiences to be classed as images rather than sensations or percepts it should be possible to show that they occur 'in the absence of those stimulus conditions that are known to produce their genuine sensory or perceptual counterparts'. Finally, behaviour that is based upon images should, typically, have 'different consequences' from behaviour based upon sensations or percepts.

The first two criteria will be designated as subjective and the second two, objective. After outlining some of the difficulties associated with both classes of criteria the chapter will conclude with a brief discussion of the relation of imaging to perceiving, remembering and thinking.

The subjective criteria

In essence the subjective criteria to be discussed refer to experienced attributes of images and sensations (or percepts) which enable us to discriminate the one from the other. The first detailed discussion of this problem is usually attributed to David Hume (1748) who argued that: 'we may divide all the perceptions of the mind into two classes or species, which are distinguished by their different degrees of force and vivacity.' 'Those perceptions, which enter with most force and violence, we may name impressions; and under this name I comprehend all our sensations, passions and emotions, . . . By ideas I mean the faint images of these in thinking and reasoning.' From David Hume to James Sully (1892) this criterion appears to have been the one that was most emphasized, though other differences were recognized, e.g., lack of stability in the image. The essential subjective distinguishing attribute of an image then, was thought to be one of quantity rather than of quality. Images as presented to us in experience are simply *less intense* than their sensory and perceptual counterparts.

Despite this tradition, Hume himself recognized that this quantitative attribute of intensity might not always serve as a distinguishing mark—'in sleep, in a fever, in madness or in any very violent emotions of soul, our ideas may approach to our impressions; as, on the other hand it sometimes happens, that our impressions are so faint and low that we cannot distinguish them from our ideas.'

Among the nineteenth century psychologists who came to doubt the adequacy of the intensity criterion was Harald Höffding (1891) who wrote: 'There is, indeed, as a rule a difference in the degree of strength of a memory image and a percept; but this difference may be very small, and may even quite disappear.' However, it was not until twenty years later that some empirical evidence against the absolute validity of the intensity criterion was provided by one of E. B. Titchener's students at Cornell University.

Using four observers and eight experimental tasks involving judgments of actual and imaged sounds, Schaub (1911) concluded that images and sensations both possessed the same attribute of intensity and that images are not always of less intensity than the original sensations on which they are based.

Instead of continuing the search for quantitative differences some psychologists towards the end of the nineteenth century proposed the alternative hypothesis that the true differences were qualitative. Images were to be thought of as differing in kind from sensations and percepts even though they might not differ in degree. For example, Titchener (1919) in an extension of Wundt's views, emphasized the textural differences between a sensation and an image. Whereas an image tends to dissolve and fade when it is fixated, a sensation or a percept tends to become more distinct. Once again, however, the distinction is not an absolute one. Some eidetic images persist for 5 or 10 minutes and may be described in great detail without dissolution or fading.

Though this criterion of stability or persistence applies under most everyday conditions, it should be emphasized that it applies chiefly to our visual experience and to a lesser extent to our auditory experience. In our contact senses of touch, taste and smell, adaptation to the stimulus occurs fairly quickly and the sensory experience ceases. Even visual perception is dependent upon some degree of change in the pattern of exitation received by the retina. If a completely stable optical image is projected on to the retina by means of special apparatus attached to the cornea, after a few seconds the pattern can no longer be seen (Pritchard, Heron and Hebb, 1960). To prevent this rapid process of visual adaptation it is necessary for the optical image to change, very slightly, its position on the retina and this is produced under natural conditions by the minute oscillatory movements of the two eyeballs.

In 1898 G. E. Stout (1907), following the ideas of his teacher James Ward, had put forward another textural difference and one which was also mentioned by Hume. He wrote:

The percept has an aggressiveness which does not belong to the image. It strikes the mind with varying degrees of force or liveliness according to the varying intensity of the stimulus. This degree of force or liveliness is part of what we ordinarily mean by the intensity of a sensation but this constituent of the intensity of sensations is absent in mental imagery.

Once again it is possible to agree that these observations may well be true in many instances, but what of the hypnagogic image? The 'aggressiveness' with which such an image impinges upon the awareness of some observers often leads to it being misperceived as having a basis in the real world of people and objects.

The definitive study which made it apparent to most psychologists that no quantitative nor qualitative attributes could serve as absolute markers for the consistent differentiation of images and percepts was conducted by Perky (1910) and recently replicated by Segal and Nathan (1964).

The basic procedure employed in both these experiments is to ask a subject to produce an image of some specified object such as a lemon or a banana and to project it on to a ground glass screen. Unbeknown to the subject this screen separates his room from another which contains a slide projector. The subject is instructed to form his image around a small fixation mark in the centre of the screen and while he is doing this a slide of the same object is projected on to the back of the screen at slightly below threshold. The intensity of illumination of the projected slide can then be raised to well above threshold without the subject becoming aware that his 'image' has any sensory basis. Though three of Perky's subjects were dropped from the analysis because procedural errors would have made their observations useless, the remaining twenty-four all accepted their percepts of the projected slides as projections of their own images, even when they expressed surprise at the unexpected size or position of the object on the screen. In the comparable part of Segal and Nathan's study six out of seven subjects responded in the same way. As these authors observe, 'there is a region of experience where the distinction between self-initiated imagery and the perception of an external event is uncertain.' What determines the magnitude of this region for any particular person is an interesting and important problem in its own right and will be discussed at greater length under the heading of 'Hallucinations' in Chapter 5. For the present it is sufficient to note that these confusions between the inner world of images and the outer world of percepts are present in individuals who are neither neurotic nor psychotic but well within the range of healthy psychological functioning.

The objective criteria

The data reported in the last section indicate how easy it is for a subject to mistake an image for a percept or a percept for an image. Is it any easier to distinguish the presence of an image from that of a percept when more objective criteria are adopted? For example, is it possible for an experimenter to assert that a subject must be experiencing a sensation or a percept of some kind, rather than an image, when he submits the subject to an external stimulus? Stout (1898) believed that such a procedure provided unequivocal evidence for the presence of a sensation or percept. He wrote: 'One characteristic mark of what we agree in calling sensation is its mode of production. It is caused by what we call a *stimulus*. A stimulus is always some condition external to the nervous system itself and operating upon it.'

It is true that what we call a stimulus will produce a sensation if it is above the detection threshold and above the attention threshold. But unfortunately the same stimulus may produce an image which is inseparably fused with the sensation. In Luria's (1960) account of Shereshevskii's synaesthesic percepts the difficulty is clearly illustrated. 'Shereshevskii himself pointed out repeatedly that sounds had for him colour and taste and were tangible; visual forms emitted sound and had a taste and so on. "What a yellow and crumbly voice you have," he told Vygotskii once.' When visual forms are experienced as emitting sounds and having a taste, what is to count as sensation and what as image? Do the properties of the visual form constitute the stimulus and only the visual experience constitute the sensation-response, or must the visual-auditory-gustatory complex be treated as a sensation-response? These synaesthesic complexes are by definition experienced as a unity, appear not to be learned in any of the usual senses of learning, and often persist unchanged and indefinitely (Langfeld, 1914). Synaesthesia can be produced experimentally with the aid of hallucinogenic drugs such as mescalin (Simpson and McKellar, 1955).

Of course the problem of what constitutes a stimulus is an old and unresolved issue in psychology, and it is not just the problem of a difference between the experimenter and the subject as to the definition of the stimulus situation. Stout said that: 'A stimulus is always some condition external to the nervous system itself and operating upon it', but when a point on the exposed temporal cortex is stimulated (Perot & Penfield, 1960) and elicits a vivid visual and auditory 're-enactment of a previous experience', does it count as a stimulus?

The problem of differentiating images from percepts by reference to the objective stimulus is further complicated by the fact that the same stimulus may lead to different reactions from the same subject on different occasions depending on his motivational set. Though this applies to situations where the stimulus is ambiguous, as in looking at an ink blot, it can also occur when the stimulus is not ambiguous but where the subject has strong needs to perceive the stimulus in a particular way. Harry Stack Sullivan (1947) gives the example of a client who after 300 hours in therapy was astounded to find that his therapist had shaved off his beard. In fact the therapist had never had a beard.

If it be argued that inference rather than true perception is involved in this example, one is, of course, faced with the problem of deciding what is to count as perception and what as inference. This is not an easy distinction either, as Russell (1927) has neatly shown.

You say, 'What can you see on the horizon?' One man says, 'I see a ship.' Another says, 'I see a steamer with two funnels.' A third says, 'I see a Cunarder going from Southampton to New York.' How much of what these three people say is to count as perception? They may all three be perfectly right in what they say, and yet we should not concede that a man can 'perceive' that the ship is going from Southampton to New York. This we should say, is inference. But it is by no means easy to draw the line; some things which are in an important sense, inferential, must be admitted to be perceptions. The man who says 'I see a ship' is using inference. Apart from experience, he only sees a queerly shaped dark dot on a blue background. Experience has taught him that that sort of dot 'means' a ship.

If it is not always possible to distinguish images from sensations or percepts on the basis of the antecedent conditions that arouse them, might it not be possible to find unequivocal differences in the consequences that follow from them? A good illustration of an argument along these lines is provided by William James (1912) who writes:

I make for myself an experience of blazing fire, I place it near my body, but it does not warm me in the least. I lay a stick upon it and the stick either burns or remains green, as I please. I call up water, and pour it on the fire, and absolutely no difference ensues. I account for all such facts by calling this whole train of experiences unreal, a mental train. Mental fire is what won't burn real sticks; mental water is what won't necessarily (though of course it may) put out even a mental fire . . . With 'real' objects, on the contrary, consequences always accrue; and thus the real experiences get sifted from the mental ones, the things from our thoughts of them, fanciful or true, and precipitated together as the stable part of the whole experience-chaos, under the name of the physical world.

As a result of experience with the differential consequences of actions based upon imaged events and perceived events we build up two separate frames of reference. As Lewin (1948) has observed, it is part of the normal process of child development for the levels of fantasy and reality to become gradually differentiated.

As we grow older any doubts that we may have concerning the reality status of an experience are confirmed or denied by reference to a wide variety of tests. If the first experience of an object is visual we may seek to touch it. If the object is a glass tumbler it should hold water if held under a running tap; it should break if thrown against a brick wall; and if I take a jagged fragment it should make a mark if I scratch it against the side of a plastic bowl. As a final check I may have recourse to asking one or more observers whether they have had similar experiences to those described. When the experience is olfactory or gustatory the distinction between percept and image is particularly difficult to make, and the use of additional observers may be our only way of doing so.

Despite the fact that it is possible for us to distinguish an image from a percept in the ways described, the very existence of paranoid delusions shows that the checking procedure does not always guarantee the making of this distinction. Once the delusion or belief is established, subsequent perceptual checks may merely result in a confirmation of the belief. The case of the psychiatrist who was trying to help a patient to overcome the delusion that the patient was dead, will serve as an illustration. After many attempts to show the man that he could not possibly be dead the psychiatrist obtained an admission that dead people don't bleed. He then took a pin from his desk and jabbed it into the back of the man's hand so that a trickle of blood flowed from the puncture. The patient looked at the blood in astonishment and exclaimed, 'Well, fancy that, dead people do bleed!'

In the everyday world of ordinary people and ordinary experiences, the belief that we have a percept rather than an image may be confirmed for us because the consequences are consistent with the belief. Yet we may be completely wrong; it may be an image after all. For example, there is good evidence to show that if we believe that an object held in the hand is hot then it not only feels hot but a measureable increase in local skin temperature occurs. In a study reported by Harano, Ogawa and Naruse (1965) it was found that under conditions of passive concentration on the phrase, 'My arms are warm', change in the felt warmth of the arms was reported and a corresponding increase in the actual temperature of the arms occurred. Related to these findings was an actual increase in blood volume as measured by a finger plethysmograph. It was also found that when an attitude of active striving was adopted to achieve this effect no subjective or objective changes in warmth occurred. This finding parallels the well-known views of Emile Coué (1922) who wrote that: 'To make good suggestions it is absolutely necessary to do it *without effort* . . . the use of the *will* . . . must be entirely put aside. One must have recourse *exclusively* to the imagination.' These observations also parallel the general view that a too active attempt to form and hold a memory image is likely to result in its dissolution.

Though an imaged fire may actually warm a person under certain conditions, it is still true that an imaged fire 'won't burn real sticks'. Though the differential consequences of imaging and of perceiving, for what happens in the 'real' world, may not always be clearly distinguished by the individual concerned, they will usually be clearly distinguished by the experimenter and his colleagues.

Discussion and conclusions

This chapter began with a formal definition of mental imagery which incorporated the main criteria by which percepts and images have been traditionally distinguished. It was the deliberate aim of the discussion that followed to emphasize some of the difficulties that exist in making this distinction absolute.

These difficulties suggest, though they don't logically imply, that some of the confusion may be due to actual similarities or partial identities in the neurological structures and proceesss involved in the two forms of experience. Oswald (1962) quite clearly holds this view; he writes: 'I believe . . . that the neurophysiological response present when a real object is perceived by means of one's sense organs, is similar to that present when an image, a pseudo-hallucination or an hallucination is perceived.' The discussion of definitional difficulties also serves to sharpen our awareness of what is likely to serve as a useful operational measure of imagery. Many measures used in the past have been introduced without sufficient awareness of the characteristics of the phenomenon to be investigated. For example McBain (1954) employs a memory for designs test as a measure of visual imagery. It has yet to be shown that an image of the design is necessary to its accurate reproduction.

To conclude this chapter and introduce the following ones some brief comments will be made on the relation of imagery to the processes of perceiving, remembering and thinking.

Both perceiving and remembering are processes which can become automatic in the sense that an appropriate response occurs immediately without any self-conscious awareness of the object perceived or remembered. Perception and memory serve us in this way most obviously when we carry through any skilled performance.

In driving a car, for example, I can be recalling the events of a football match. Yet my behaviour will show that I am perceiving all the car-driving-relevant-events and that other information is being supplied by my memory store which causes me, for example, to reduce speed at a spot where I have previously encountered a driving hazard. Under these circumstances I am unlikely to be self-consciously aware of either the percepts or images relevant to my car driving behaviour. However, when perceiving and remembering cease to be automatic because some unfamiliar situation presents itself, we try to become more aware of the specific, relevant, concrete events in our perceptual field and in our memory store.

How are we able to dwell on our percepts so that they persist unchanged long enough for appropriate actions to be taken? A short-term perceptual-memory store of the kind to be discussed under the heading of memory after imagery and eidetic imagery would seem to serve this function. The younger the person the more likely it is that he will encounter totally unfamiliar objects and events and the greater will be the potential value of a short-term perceptual-memory store for him. As we grow older the capacity of this store appears to be drastically limited, even in those who once possessed a relatively large capacity. For example, Sperling's (1960) research, which is discussed in the next chapter, implies that in the average adult the visual perceptual-memory store has a very limited capacity and an effective duration of less than one second.

Many writers (e.g. Werner, 1948; Bruner, Olver and Greenfield, 1966) have pointed to imagery as the significant basis of cognitive operations in children. With the emergence of more schematic and linguistically based cognitive processes the role of imagery begins to decline in the majority of children who live in modern industrialized societies. For this reason the persistence of vivid sensory imagery into adult life is rare and the memory image, when it exists at all, is typically a schematic reconstruction of something seen rather than a full bodied re-presentation. The extent to which the more vivid imagery of childhood can be reinstated in the adult is one of the problems associated with imagination imagery and appears to have some association with those processes to which we apply the general term 'creative thinking'. Though thinking, of a problem-solving variety, may make use of memory images as concrete elements in the process of achieving a solution, imagination imagery, as its name suggests, typically has a novel quality which may even surprise its possessor. It is this novel quality which sometimes provides the original idea for the solution to a problem or for the creation of a work of art.

Chapter 2

AFTER-IMAGERY

OF ALL the forms of imagery to be discussed that of after-imagery is most dependent upon the actual conditions of sensory stimulation, and in its usual manner of arousal is least dependent upon processes at the cortical level.

Most people have at some time become aware of a *visual* after-image and because it is such a common phenomenon and one which is relatively easy to study experimentally, it is not surprizing to find that most research has been directed toward it.

By comparison with the visual mode, very few investigations have been concerned with after-imagery in other modalities. Boring (1942) provides only a very brief discussion of this phenomenon as it occurs in relation to pressure, temperature and vestibular stimulation. Pressure and vestibular after-images are common in the experience of most people. The normal pressure accompanying the wearing of a hat seems to persist for some time after it has been removed and the apparent movement of the solid ground is a normal sequel to several hours of rocking in a small boat, but little research has been undertaken to study the necessary and sufficient conditions for their occurrence.

Until recently the only auditory phenomenon that might have qualified as an after-image is the persistent ringing in the ears (tinnitus) that follows exposure to deafening sounds. However, this has been likened to the visual phenomenon of 'spots before the eyes' and has not been generally accepted as an auditory after-image. Rosenblith and his colleagues (1947) at the Harvard Psycho-accoustic Laboratory have reported an unusual auditory after-effect which, they believe, should be considered for after imagery status. They found that if a person is stimulated for at least 20 seconds with auditory pulses of 120 microseconds duration and at a frequency of between 30 and 200 pulses per second there is a striking change in the quality of familiar sounds heard immediately afterwards. A handclap, a typewriter, the human voice, scraping sandpaper, all sound metallic. Listeners describe the effect as 'jangly', 'twangy', 'like a rasping file'. The duration of this after-effect increases as a function of exposure time and intensity of stimulation, e.g., about 4 seconds duration after an exposure of 25 seconds to a pulse intensity of 125 db., or about 11 seconds after an exposure of 160 seconds at the same intensity. If no sound follows the pulse stimulation period then the subject experiences nothing but silence.

As might be expected, most interest has been shown in the conditions that influence the formation and course of the visual after-image in both its positive and negative forms and it is with the problem of the peripherally produced visual after-image that I want to begin. Having shown that retinal stimulation is *sufficient* to evoke an after-image the next section contains a review of evidence for and against the hypothesis that centrally initiated stimulation may also be *sufficient* to evoke an after-image. The phenomenon of recurrent imagery is then discussed as it seems to depend upon prolonged retinal stimulation, but at the same time it is influenced by central processes. The chapter is concluded with a discussion of the after-image as a short term memory store and the term memory after-image has been resurrected to describe this function.

Peripheral stimulation as a sufficient condition

Positive after-images, in which the effects of a black and white or coloured stimulus persist as an after-image with the same relative brightness and colour relations after the stimulus has been removed, occur most readily when the stimulus has been of high intensity and brief duration and when the subsequent projection field is relatively dark. A good example is provided by the nearby flash of lightning which leaves behind it a positive after-image as one continues to look into the night.

The typical course of the positive after-image is a short one. Within a few seconds it fades and is then replaced by a negative after-image. However, a phenomenon known as the 'flight of colours' (Külpe, 1893; Berry, 1922, 1927; Berry and Imus, 1935) may occur if the eye is first stimulated by a bright white light in a completely dark room. With a totally black projection field a sequence of colours is reported in the after-image. Though this sequence may be influenced by a variety of pre- and post-stimulating conditions, and no fixed sequence has ever been established, Woodworth (1939) concluded that yellow is 'the predominant colour in the early part of the sequence with red commonly following, then blue or purple and finally, in many cases, dark green'. A positive after-image is usually explained as a persistence of the electro-chemical effects produced in the retina by the original stimulus, but a more exact statement is still waiting upon future research (Brown, 1965). Prolonged positive after-images have often been regarded as an indication of eidetic ability (e.g. Meenes and Morton, 1936). It is also known that the duration of an after-image is longer if the original stimulation is limited to the fovea.

All visual after-images are literally seen as a percept is seen, but unlike a normal percept or an eidetic-image they move with the movement of the eyes. This occurs whether the eyes are open and the image is projected on to some adjacent surface or whether the eyes are closed and observed against a background of retinal grey.

Negative after-images in which the black and white areas of the original stimulus are seen as reversed, or where the colours of the original stimulus are seen as complementary, are obtained under several different sets of conditions.

For example, in a recent study by Sperling (1960a) a tachistoscope was used to expose a white card containing black letters (20 milliseconds at 70 foot-lamberts) followed immediately by a homogeneous white field (75 milliseconds at 22 foot-lamberts). Under these conditions the subject reports seeing 'bright *white* letters, clear and distinct, on a less white background'. Positive after-images were not reported by any subjects in this experiment. Of particular interest was the finding that a continually flickering negative after-image could be maintained indefinitely by arranging for the cycle of exposures to be repeated automatically.

Though after-images are easy enough to produce, their attributes (e.g. clarity and duration) are influenced by a wide

15

variety of variables. Among the more important stimulus conditions are the following: intensity, duration, size and position of the optical image on the retina, and hue. As might be expected the after-image is also affected by the hue and brightness of the projection field. Subject conditions such as the steadiness of fixation on the original stimulus and the degree of prior dark adaptation are also of importance. Relatively little work has been done on more consistent and habitual individual differences though, as noted earlier, there is some evidence to suggest that eidetikers have more persistent positive after-images.

The use of long fixation times (5 to 60 seconds) was common in the nineteenth century, but eye movements introduced an unknown degree of influence on the results, and modern workers prefer to use higher intensities and fixation times of about one second.

Reliable data on many functional relations between, e.g., duration of the after-image and such variables as period of prior dark adaptation, stimulus duration and stimulus intensity have now been obtained (e.g., Feinbloom, 1938).

Of special importance in the study of after imagery, as in the study of most other forms of imagery, is the provision of adequate training in recognition, examination and report of the phenomenon. As Woodworth (1938) points out: 'Many students require some practice before seeing the after-image, because it is one of those subjective phenomena which our whole practical life leads us to disregard.'

In a study by Reinhold (1957) it was found that the mean number of seconds required to become aware of after-images declined significantly over a series of sixteen trials.

At the beginning of this chapter it was asserted that of all forms of imagery the after-image was most dependent upon the actual conditions of sensory stimulation and least dependent upon cortical processes. It will now be appropriate to cite the nature of the evidence for the sufficiency of retinal processes in accounting for the attributes of after-imagery, but other evidence will be discussed which suggests that cortical processes may also be involved under some circumstances.

The evidence indicating that retinal processes are sufficient to account for an after-image may be illustrated from the work of Craik (1940).

When the optic nerve has been briefly paralysed to eliminate cortical involvement, a bright light to that eye will still be followed by a clear negative after-image. Temporary blindness can be induced by pressing downward on the top of the half closed eyelid. Pressure must be maintained while the now blinded eye is exposed for about 2 minutes to the primary stimulus. Craik used a 60-watt bulb and obtained a stable image by allowing the normal eye to fixate this primary stimulus. About 10 seconds after the pressure is released a slightly blurred and less intense after-image is seen with the previously blinded eye. Because inter-ocular effects are possible when the normal eye remains open, it is important to note that an after-image is still obtained when the normal eye is closed.

Craik's finding was confirmed by Oswald (1957) who also demonstrated that under conditions of pressure blindness a negative after-image could be obtained to a coloured stimulus.

These results provide a reasonable basis for believing that stimulus conditions at the retina are sufficient to account for *some* after-images. That stimulus conditions at the retina are not sufficient to account for *all* after-images is suggested by a number of investigators who have studied the so-called Bocci image. In some people, by no means all, the monocular fixation of a bright stimulus for approximately 30 seconds can result in the development of an after-image in the unstimulated eye. This phenomenon appears to have been known at least since the time of Newton (cited by Day, 1958) but was independently discovered by the Italian psychologist B. Bocci in 1900 (cited by Sumner and Watts, 1936). More recently it has been the subject of investigation by two Japanese psychologists Ohwaki and Kihara (1953). These workers report that this form of after-image is like the eidetic-image in being fairly common in children up to the age of 12 years. It is infrequently found among adolescents and is even rare among adults. In children between the ages of 7 and 12 the Bocci image is positively coloured and is of considerably longer duration than the corresponding monocular after-image of the stimulated eye. However, there is evidence that if one eye is stimulated for about 60 seconds by a small colour patch placed on a black ground, and subsequently the non-stimulated eye is fixated upon a white projection field, most people will see a *negative* after-image. This after-image differs from the after-image in the stimulated eye in several says, e.g., it is slightly smaller and fainter (Sumner and Watts, 1936).

Central stimulation as a sufficient condition

The question to be considered now is whether positive evidence can be found to support the view that central processes alone might be sufficient to produce a visual after-image in the complete absence of any external source of visual stimulation.

As early as 1812 (cited by Oswald, 1957) it was reported by Gruithuisen that on awakening from sleep he had counted more than 100 occasions on which negative after-images had been experienced on the basis of prior dream images. More recently Leaning (1926) reports the experience of a Mrs Drummond who dreamed of a beautiful two-handled vase 'which was green in the dream drawing room where she saw it, but showed red on reclosing her eyes after waking'. However, it is difficult to evaluate this evidence as it is known (Wood-worth, 1938) that after-images are more readily formed and are of longer duration when the eye has been rested by sleep, and the possibility exists that an intense visual stimulus during early-morning light sleep might serve as the basis of a dream image and also of the subsequent after-image.

In 1863 Wundt himself stated that the prolonged contemplation of a brightly coloured mental image with one's eyes closed will result in a brief negative after-image when the eyes are opened and the gaze is directed on to a plain white surface. Several investigators (Downie, 1901; Weiskrantz, 1950; Oswald, 1957) have carried out investigations of this phenomenon with waking subjects and have obtained some supporting evidence. All three investigators report that the spontaneous after-images to the imaged stimuli persisted for about 5 seconds, which is a considerably shorter duration than is usually obtained under conditions of direct retinal stimulation. Sutcliffe (1962) found that not only were the reported after-images of brief duration when they appeared, but that after-images to imaged colours developed more slowly than those obtained with real stimuli. However one of Oswald's subjects was exceptional in that his after-image to an imaged stimulus lasted between 30 and 45 seconds (Oswald, 1959). The after-imagery of this man appeared 'spontaneously and *effortlessly*' and after about 5 seconds it 'began to pulsate, going rapidly in and out and thus gradually shrinking smaller and smaller till it disappeared. This pulsation was not present in the primary image and was only faintly perceptible in the after-images of real visual patterns.' These fluctuations in size corresponded to the rhythm of the man's arterial pulse. It is known that blood pressure changes correspond to change in the excitation level of impulse from the reticular formation. Oswald interprets the rhythmic changes in the phenomenal appearance of the after-image as due to changes in levels of awareness induced by these changes in output from the reticular formation.

Most of these observations seem to provide support for the hypothesis that central processes alone might be sufficient to produce an after-image. However, an alternative hypothesis that would account for most of these supporting observations is that they result from the implicit expectations of the experimenter and of his subjects.

Martin Orne (1962) has used the term 'demand characteristics' to describe all such expectations as they affect the subject's behaviour in an experimental situation. Knowing the elementary text book facts concerning the negative after-image may influence some subjects to report that they see what they believe they are supposed to see.

This alternative hypothesis is given some support from the results of a review by Barber (1964) of those studies which have made use of hypnotized rather than waking subjects. Of the ten studies reviewed six obtained negative or equivocal results and only four obtained positive results. Barber writes:

Additional research is needed to reconcile the contradictions in the above investigations. It is imperative, however, that further experiments in this area institute very stringent selection procedures to exclude the possibility that Ss may have knowledge of negative after-images. That this possibility may not have been excluded in the investigations presenting positive findings is indicated by the following. The 'correct' after-images reported by Ss participating in the Binet and Féré, Erickson and Erickson, Rosenthal and Mele, and Barber experiments were consistent with the negative after-image phenomenon as it is described in elementary psychology textbooks, but they were not consistent with the negative after-image phenomenon as it is actually observed in real life. These Ss almost always reported green as the after-image of hallucinated red, blue as the after-image of hallucinated yellow, and vice versa.

Barber then goes on to note that wide individual differences occur in the description of after-images produced by actual coloured stimuli, and that untrained subjects are often unable to see their after-images at the first attempt. Since subjects taking part in the four studies reporting positive results . . .

. . . tended to describe the after-images in a textbook fashion and showed very little intra-and inter-individual variations in their descriptions, they may have previously read elementary textbook accounts of the negative after-image and were able during the experiment, to surmise what responses were expected from them.

Among the procedures that might be used to determine whether the phenomenon is ever a genuine one might be the selection of naïve subjects such as children or members of pre-literate societies, and the use of additional procedures based upon the manipulation of conditions known to influence phenomenal experience of ordinary after-images.

For example, Weiskrantz (1950) found that his S obtained after-images to an imaged black square, which varied in size according to predictions based on Emmert's Law. He notes also that: 'the "real" series was not conducted until the "imaginary" series had been completed and that the random orders were different in the two series.' To check whether the size of an after-image could be *guessed* with the same degree of accuracy, Weiskrantz used a graduate student in psychology who was familiar with Emmert's Law and who also had qualifications in physics. The size of the 'after-image' supposed to be at different projection distances diverged widely from the sizes predictable on the basis of Emmert's Law.

Three further observations which suggest that after-images to imagined stimuli may occur spontaneously in some subjects but not in others, come from the work of Perky (1910) Jaensch (1930) and Purdy (1936). Findings reported by these investigators imply that the subject must be able to achieve a 'vivid' image of the stimulus if an after-image is to develop. Perky found that her subjects occasionally obtained after-images to the more vivid imagination images but not to the relatively weaker memory images. These results are of especial interest because they were quite incidental to the main investigation. In the work of Jaensch it was reported that an eidetic subject could obtain a negative after-image to an eidetically imaged colour square. Purdy's subject was a girl aged 21 who was tested during her senior year at the University. She had possessed eidetic ability for as long as she could remember and had not ever thought that it was in any way unusual. When asked to imagine the appearance of the sun's disk,

She reports a glaringly bright image which refuses to disappear for several minutes. She declares that this image causes her eyes to water and to smart. As the image fades it turns into a purple disk with a white rim.

This also, was an incidental finding to which Purdy comments, that it 'is suggestive of the after-images that one obtains from the actual sun'.

One possibility of providing an objective check on the validity of after-images to imagined stimuli is suggested by the studies of Jasper and Cruickshank (1937) and Drewes (1958). Both these studies report alpha blocking to a genuine after-image. Drewes observed that . . .

. . . in some instances when the visual stimulus consisted of looking intently for a few seconds at a bright light that the latency period before *complete* return of the alpha rhythm, when the eyes were closed again, was three or four seconds longer than usual.

Though the task of interpreting alpha suppression is not a simple one (see chapter 4, this volume) future research on the problems discussed in this section might well utilize the electroencephalograph.

Finally, there is the possibility of demonstrating the sufficiency of central processes in the production of after-imagery by using a conditioning procedure. If an after-image to a bright light is regularly paired with an auditory signal can it be shown that the sound alone is capable of producing an after-image? Brown (1965) quotes a series of experimental investigations by Popov and Popov (1953, 1954) as providing provisional support for the possibility of conditioning after-images, but a careful reading of the original reports casts some doubt on whether this interpretation of the Popov's experiments is justified.

Recurrent imagery

A subjective visual experience that is familiar to many people, but which is readily distinguishable from most of the preceding forms of after-imagery is the recurrent visual image. Several names have been used to describe these experiences; for example, Ward (1883) calls them 'recurrent sensations' while Warren (1921) uses the term 'delayed after-sensations' and Oswald (1962) refers to them as 'perseverative images'. Hanawalt (1954) has called them 'recurrent images' and it is this latter name that has been adopted throughout the present discussion.

According to Ward (1883) the nineteenth century German anatomist F. G. J. Henle was the first person to call attention to the phenomenon. He noted that after working with a microscope all day the objects he had been viewing would often appear vividly before him in the dark some hours later. Though recurrent images occur after prolonged and intense stimulation in other sensory modalities, especially the auditory and kinaesthetic, it is once again in the visual mode that the experience is most commonly reported.

The following detailed description is typical and comes from Hanawalt (1954).

After a family excursion into a blackberry patch, my wife reported to me as she closed her eyes after retiring that she could see beautiful blackberries, just perfect for picking, hanging in great profusion on bushes. Upon closing my eyes I discovered that I too saw them. The images greatly impressed me for they were neither after-images in the usual sense, nor were they memory images. The images were positive and appeared to be located in the eyes rather than projected. They were very vivid; they could be *seen* not just imagined as in the case of memory images. In this respect they were like the usual after-image. Introspectively they appeared to be retinal phenomenon. The berry-picking excursion occurred during a bright sunny day about eight hours before we retired. My wife and I both saw idealized images; the berries were large, purple tinged, luscious and profuse. In place of the almost prohibitive brier patch, the berries hung upon open shoots; they were easily accessible and all of them were ripe. During the excursion we had seen many small berries, green berries, and bird pecked berries, but in our images not an imperfect berry appeared. The background was present but subdued in comparision to the berries. The green leaves of the bushes were seen but greatly reduced in number and saturation.

Though the circumstances in which these visual recurrent images appear might lead to them being called hypnagogic images the antecedent conditions of prolonged and intense retinal stimulation makes them a distinctive phenomenon and in this respect more like the after-image. However, it is clear that interaction between peripheral stimulating conditions and central processes is involved in these recurrent images. Most observers are aware of the differences between the original sequence of perceptual experiences and the sequence of re-current images. The 'idealized images' reported by Hanawalt provides an illustration of this. After a day's strawberry picking another psychologist, Margaret Sutherland, wrote of her recurrent imagery: 'It was extremely vivid, in glowing colours (red and green of course); a formal pattern of strawberry and leaf alternating' (quoted by McKellar, 1957). To what extent do motivational influences account for the 'idealized images' and the 'formal patterns'; to what extent do entoptic pheno-mena play a part and to what extent is it a function of repeated exposure to different examples of the same class of object. In one study of eidetic imagery it was found that an 'idealized image' of a leaf resulted when a series of seven differently shaped leaves had been previously presented one at a time. Such reports are similar to the results of experiments on com-posite photography (Galton 1883) where, for example, the heads of four or five women may be photographed in the same position on the one negative producing an idealized woman. Again experiments in which a stereoscope has been used to present a different full-face photograph to each eye can result in a fusion of the two which is typically experienced as more attractive than either face when seen alone.

It might have been expected that the recurrent image would have received more attention from the experimental psycho-logist, but no studies have been found that directly bear upon the effects of prolonged, variable and intense stimulation of the eyes. However, Swindle (1916, 1917) has provided an idea which might serve as a guide to a preliminary investigation. He writes (1916),

I once illuminated a person in a dark room and observed a distinct positive after-image of him. We then went into a well illuminated room and talked for about forty minutes. I then went alone into the dark room, remained about ten minutes and then with *closed* eyes illuminated the room once more (a single illumination) and imme-diately I observed a distinct positive after-image of many seconds duration of the person whom I had previously fixated. Several of my subjects have had analagous experiences.

Memory after-imagery

The question to be considered concerns the possibility of storing accurate information for the brief time that a positive after-image persists. Because the focus of inquiry is upon the storage or retention of information it will be convenient to use the late nineteenth century term memory after-image, or primary memory image as it was sometimes called.

In 1883 James Ward wrote,

The primary memory image can always be obtained, and is obtained to most advantage, by looking intently at some object for an instant and then closing the eyes or turning them away. The object is then imaged for a moment very vividly and distinctly, and can be so recovered several times by an effort of attention . . . The primary memory image retains so much of its original definiteness and intensity as to make it possible with great accuracy to compare two physical phenomena, one of which is in this way remembered while the other is really present; for the most part this is indeed a more accurate procedure than that of dealing with both together. But this is only possible for a very short time. From Weber's experiment with weights and lines it would appear that even after 10 seconds a considerable waning has taken place, and after 100 seconds all that is distinctive of the primary image has probably ceased.

The ability which Ward describes is not as common as he implies and may perhaps be related to the capacity for eidetic imaging. However, Klüver (1926) reports a somewhat similar experience after ingesting 23 grammes of powdered peyote (mescal buttons). He writes,

The stimulus material was placed before me in a darkened room and then suddenly illuminated for one second or less . . . *Stimulus*: picture of a tiger: yellow with black stripes and black contour. I do not know what picture is placed before me in the dark. *After-image*: my right hand holding the picture of the tiger; the texture of my coat, the shirt, folds on my thumb quite clear; the picture of the tiger itself in brilliant yellow with deep black contour and stripes.

Most subjects do experience a memory after-image if the object is illuminated by a brief and brilliant flash under background conditions of total darkness. With such a brief exposure no appreciable movement of the eye in relation to the object is possible and an after-image of great clarity and detail can result. In a study by Gregory, Wallace and Campbell (1959), using a 110 joule 1 milli-second flash tube, positive after-images of several seconds duration were produced. In one instance it was found that the flash illumination of a corridor produced an after-image which changed in perspective as the subject moved.

This latter phenomenon is easy to replicate for oneself using an ordinary photographer's flash gun. If one is in a dark room, facing a chair at a distance of about 10 feet when the flash occurs, it is possible, for example, to walk towards a point 2 or 3 feet to the left of the chair and to observe the imaged chair from a constantly changing angle as one approaches it.

Brindley (1962) has also shown that a brief but very bright illumination of a simple grating pattern, when allowed to fall upon the fovea, can still be seen clearly 1 or 2 minutes later. It appears that the loss of resolution (blurring) that occurs in the following minutes is not due to a gradual fading of the after-image. Speed of blurring was measured roughly by the time it takes for the after-image to become so blurred that it is impossible to recognize the direction of the bars in the grating pattern. If a weak stimulus flash is employed, fine detail (grating pattern with bars subtending 1' of arc at the eye) can be resolved for almost as long as the after-image continues to be visible. With a more intense stimulus, and therefore a more enduring after-image, even coarse detail (grating patterns with bars subtending 10' of arc at the eye) becomes completely blurred long before the after-image disappears.

Interest in the information storage capacity of the retina has led to a series of ingenious experiments by Sperling (1960, 1963) in which the subject is given an instructional set at varying periods after the stimulus pattern has been illuminated for 50 milliseconds.

A typical stimulus display consists of two or three rows of consonants having either three or four to a row. The subject is then trained to report the letters in one or other of these rows according to a prearranged signal. A post-stimulus high tone (2500 cps) was used to indicate that the top row should be reported; a medium range tone (650 cps) served as a cue for the middle line and a low tone (250 cps) for the bottom one.

As might be expected if the signal is given even as short a time as 5 milliseconds before the stimulus is exposed the subjects are able to report the letters without error, but if the signal is delayed until a full second after exposure then the average accuracy drops by about one-third. A dark post-stimulus field produced more accurate reports than a white one but the order of reporting letters and the linear position of the letters to be reported had no effect on accuracy. In fact Sperling's (1960) main conclusion was that accuracy is chiefly dependent 'on the ability of the observer to read a visual image that persists for a fraction of a second after the stimulus has been turned off'.

A comparable form of memory after imagery in the auditory mode has sometimes been reported. A recent example will be cited from a self report by Rimland (1964) which appears in his book on autistic children:

The incident occurred while I was deeply engrossed in reading. Some time had passed before I became aware that someone had asked me a question and was awaiting a response. My mind was quite blank. I had no idea what I had been asked. I was about to ask that the question be repeated when this suddenly became un-necessary. I could hear the query, phrased in two short but complete sentences, being repeated word for word, the 'sound' coming from within my head. The effect was that of an echo, except that several seconds, perhaps as many as ten, had passed. The experience was not unfamiliar, though never before had it been so vivid.

He noted two characteristics of this experience; first, that the question had been sensed and recorded without awareness and without interpretation, second, that though the echo-like voice was identifiably that of the person who asked the question it had 'a high pitched, hollow, wooden sound'.

This quality of the human voice under these conditions has a resemblance to the auditory after-effects reported by Rosenblith et al (1947) and discussed earlier in this chapter. Investigation of the Rosenblith phenomenon with autistic children might reveal important clues to the nature of their auditory experience.

Informal inquiry among his friends suggested to Rimland that this auditory form of a memory after-image and the qualities of the echo-like voice were not uncommon. What particularly interested him were the similarities between this occasional way of functioning in normal adults and the regular way of functioning found in autistic children. The autistic child appears not to be attending, yet information is retained and recalled without apparent understanding or change in content. This literal repetition of what has been heard earlier is also said to be common among *idiot savants*.

The occurrence of isolated areas of extraordinary mental ability in individuals showing a low order of ability in all other areas does fit the picture of autism very well. *Idiot savants* have been noted with special abilities in calculation, music, art, mechanics, mental calendar manipulation, and memory. This list applies very well to the autistic child's often-reported special interests and abilities.

While information is apparently registered and retrieved without loss or alteration the autistic child fails to develop associative links between the items of information that are stored. The distressing consequence of this failure is an absence of normal conceptual development.

The weight of the evidence is regarded by Rimland as 'highly consistent with expectation based on organic pathology'. This is not, of course, an assertion that all autism is caused by a primary organic condition, but it is interesting to compare the concrete memory processes of the autistic child with the somewhat similar eidetic imaging of the brain injured children reported by Siipola and Hayden (1965) and discussed in the next chapter.

As there is evidence of a lower CFF in the aged than in the mature adult and in those with brain injury compared with normal subjects (see Zlody, 1965) the systematic examination of CFF in relation to the memory after-image, eideticism and autism would seem to be an important area of future research.

However, the primary organic basis hypothesis should not be overworked nor considered apart from other factors that may play a part. Neither a strong literal or rote memory nor the presence of specialized gifts in music or mathematics need be divorced from a high level of general intelligence. Some account must also be given of the Einsteins of this world (Hadamard, 1954) who appear to possess both high abstract ability as well as the capacity for concrete quasi-sensory modes of thought.

The ability to form eidetic-images has been mentioned in

several places in this chapter. It is now time to consider what is known about eideticism in more detail. Though clearly a different phenomenon, the term memory after-image has sometimes (e.g. Allport, 1924) been used to describe what would now be called an eidetic-image.

Chapter 3

EIDETIC IMAGERY

IN 1909 the German psychologist E. R. Jaensch coined the word *eidetic* (from the Greek eidos—that which is seen) to describe a form of percept-like imagery differing from after-imagery by persisting longer and not requiring a fixed gaze for its formation. It can occur in relation to a complex stimulus pattern and its vivid details are described in the present tense while being seen projected on some external surface. The colouring of this image is always positive and even the after-image to a small homogenous colour patch is typically positive for the eidetic individual.

This chapter begins with an account of how interest in eidetic imagery developed. After reviewing some of the main characteristics of the phenomenon and some of the problems associated with its measurement, the chapter concludes with a discussion of its functional significance.

Historical background

In a discussion of some early observers of subjective visual phenomena Heinrich Klüver (1926) cites Johannes Evangelista Purkinje as the first person to give a careful description of the visual eidetic-image as early as 1819. It seems probable that it is this same phenomenon that was called 'subjective vision' by Johannes Müller in 1826 and 'imaginary perception' by Alfred Binet in 1899.

The first empirical investigations were reported in 1907 by V. Urbantschitsch who also deserves credit for noting that these images were primarily a phenomenon of childhood.

However, he believed that these 'perceptual memory images' as he called them, were not altogether a normal phenomenon but one which tended to occur in more 'excitable' children.

After Jaensch had rechristened these perceptual memory images in 1909 little further attention was paid to them until 1917 when Otto Kroh, who was teaching in a Marburg high school reported that visual eidetic imagery was relatively common in normal school children. This event inaugurated the long series of investigations undertaken by the Jaensch brothers and their students at the Marburg Institute for Psychology. The next ten years produced a massive literature and represents one of the liveliest periods of concentrated research on a single topic in the whole history of experimental psychology. Enthusiasm was so strong that in 1924 Otto Klemm wrote that the discovery of eidetic ability ranked first among 'the true advances of psychology in the last decade' (cited by Klüver, 1926).

Though Allport (1924, 1928) and Klüver (1926, 1928, 1931, 1932) together with Jaensch (1930) made the literature on eidetic imagery readily available to the English-speaking world, only a handful of empirical investigations have been published in the psychology journals of England and the United States in the past forty years.

Sporadic interest continued, but until the publication of Haber and Haber's (1964) paper only two papers of theoretical interest appeared in the journals. Both of these in effect denied that eidetic imagery is a unique and distinctive form of imagery. Morsh and Abbot (1947) concluded their study by writing: 'The eidetic-image is merely a vivid after-image, due probably to persistence of activity in the retina', and Traxel (1962) working with children in the primary schools of Marburg itself concluded that so-called eidetic imagery when it is reported can be attributed to a combination of efficient retention, vivid memory images and suggestion.

These two studies appear to differ more in the interpretation of facts than in the facts themselves. This is particularly true of the study by Morsh and Abbott in which a small subgroup had sufficiently distinctive qualities to be categorized as eidetic by the criteria used by Haber and Haber (1964). This subgroup has been shown in Table 3.1 for comparison with the results of two other studies.

Additional characteristics of eidetic imagery

Almost all investigators have commented upon the *clarity* of the detail in an eidetic-image and the fact that it is seen in the same sense as a percept is seen. If a person has an eidetic-image before him he will turn his eyes to the relevant spot if asked to report upon a particular detail or even lift up the projection mat to obtain a better look. An after-image examined in this way will normally disappear from the field of view. The eidetic-image *persists* for longer periods than the after-image and can be recovered at will by many eidetikers even weeks (Doob, 1965) or years later (Luria, 1960) though little has been reported concerning the accuracy of these later reconstructions.

This *external localization* of the image is said to occur even when the eyes are closed. The eidetic image is never localized within the head.

The normal after-image has been said to approximate Emmert's law. If the original stimulus is fixated at a distance of 30 centimetres and forms an image on the retina 1 centimetre in diameter, then the projected after-image will measure approximately 2 centimetres at 60 centimentres distance or 4 centimetres at 120 centimetres. It is doubtful whether this 'law' is true, even of after-images, but Klüver (1926) asserted that an approximation to Emmert's law will be found most commonly at projection distances between 50 and 100 centimetres. However, Meenes and Morton (1936) could find no support for this assertion, even when a simple homogeneous stimulus was fixated.

If the original stimulus object is three-dimensional it has been observed that for some subjects the image will also appear in appropriate colours and in three dimensions. It has even been reported (Purdy, 1936) that completely realistic three-dimensional images were obtained by one subject when two-dimensional pictures were used as stimuli. This author also quotes an interesting incident described by Jaensch, who wrote:

A distinguished scholar who possesses strong eidetic images once told me that he has always been secretly amused to see people look at stereoscopic pictures, because he himself can obtain from any simple photograph or postcard a picture that is like reality in solidity and in size as well, and the illusion-value of this picture is not increased by using that 'ridiculous apparatus'.

Because so many of the attributes of an eidetic-image typically correspond to those of the original percept on which it is based, it is not surprizing that the term 'photographic memory' has often been identified with the eidetic-image. But like all memory processes, the eidetic-image is subject to the influence of motivational states and changes in the stimulus context. In some eidetic subjects no image may be formed at all if the content of the picture stimulus does not interest them. Allport (1924) refers to studies by Otto Kroh in which half the eidetic subjects failed to achieve an eidetic-image after looking at the picture, of a house whereas all of them obtained images to a picture of a monkey. Purdy (1936) also reports on a subject who found it difficult to obtain eidetic-images when nonsense figures were used as stimuli. Though interest and attention cannot be ignored, Allport (1924) found that three of his thirty 11-year old children could spell the word *Gartenwirthschaft* either forward or backward even though they knew no German and the word was merely printed above a shop as part of a fairly complex street scene. However, these same subjects were said to have control over their images to a remarkable extent:

. . . a carriage was made to drive away, turn a corner in the road, and so to disappear entirely from the image. People could be made to enter and leave and to perform *normal* actions. The range of flexibility is very great indeed, but it does not extend to include the ridiculous or unnatural.

More explorations of this last assertion is required to discover whether the imaginative child for whom more things are possible would be limited in this way. As it stands the assertion implies perhaps that the subjects used were functioning in the concrete manner described by Goldstein and Scheerer (1941). The findings of Siipola and Hayden (1965) indicate that eidetic ability is more likely to be present in a population of brain-injured children than in a population of normal children or even in a population of non-brain-injured, but feeble minded, children. The observation by Urbantschitsch that eideticism seemed to be associated with 'excitable' children also would be consistent with the presence of brain injury. More recently

Freides and Hayden (1966) have reported three cases in which eideticism occurs in one eye only. Their preliminary findings suggest that this unilateral eidetic imagery is related to brain damage in the contralateral hemisphere.

Another example of eidetic-images in which parts of the picture are seen to move is provided by Klüver (1926). One of the test pictures contained a donkey standing at some distance from a manger. If Klüver suggested that the donkey was hungry some of his eidetic subjects were surprised to see the donkey move to the manger and start to eat. These movements and altered details are said to be seen as vividly as any of the original features in the picture.

Measuring eidetic imagery

In testing for eidetic imagery the subject is usually encouraged to inspect the stimulus picture just as he would in looking at any new object in his environment. This scanning approach distinguishes the formation of an eidetic-image from that of an after-image.

Allport (1924) found that an exposure time of 35 seconds produced the best results, but this does not seem to be crucial. Good results have been obtained by Meenes and Morton (1936) using a 10 second exposure, by Teasdale (1934) using 20 seconds, by Haber and Haber (1964) using 30 seconds and by Morsh and Abbott (1945) using 40 seconds.

From the time of Jaensch silhouette pictures in black and white have provided the most common stimulus but coloured pictures of good contrast are also used.

When the subject has been exposed to the stimulus picture for the period allotted, the picture is removed and the subject is asked to report on anything that he sees on the projection mat. Though the latency of image formation is usually no more than a few seconds it may take up to 60 seconds to develop in some eidetic subjects.

Even when the image develops fairly quickly, it seldom happens that all the details of the stimulus picture will appear at once. Different parts of the image develop at different rates (Klüver, 1930) and also tend to fade at different rates. This latter observation is of interest in relation to a report by Bennett-Clark and Evans (1963) on after-images to patterned targets. They exposed five subjects to four different forms of black and white target. Each target was illuminated from behind by using a flash bulb set in a reflector. Clear, brilliant, positive after-images (memory after-images?) of long duration were produced by this method. Different parts of the image faded unpredictably at different rates. Only occasionally did the whole pattern fade out all of a piece. After an indefinite interval the image would reappear often as a total pattern, but sometimes as a part only. A possible explanation of this 'fragmentation' effect has been suggested by Freides and Hayden (1966) on the basis of their discovery that unilateral eidetic imagery can occur. When an eidetic-image is being formed in relation to one eye but not in relation to the other, a binocular rivalry situation could be created which could make possible the suppression of part or all of the image when the original stimulus picture was removed.

Since the early days of the Marburg investigations it has been common practice to prepare subjects for their eidetic imagery test by first presenting a test of after-imagery. In this way the subject obtains a preliminary experience of one kind of 'seen' imagery. Allport (1928) and Klüver (1932) have suggested that this procedure might set the subject to see eidetic-images as externally localized. To check on this possibility Meenes and Morton (1936) tested for eidetic imagery before testing for after-imagery but no difference in localization was reported. However, the fact that subjects were asked what they 'saw on the projection screen' could by itself produce externally localized images.

In the study by Haber and Haber (1964) complete data were obtained from 151 boys and girls from an elementary school in Newhaven, Connecticut. The ages of these children ranged from 7 to 12 years.

When a subject entered the test room he was seated at a distance of 20 inches from a 24 x 30 inches, neutral grey easel. A narrow ledge at the bottom was used to support each of the eight test cards.

In the after-imagery test, four coloured squares (red, blue, black and yellow) of 2 inch sides were mounted on 10 x 12 inch boards and exposed one at a time for a period of 10 seconds. The subjects were instructed to stare hard at each square without moving their eyes. After each card was removed they

34

were instructed to continue looking at the neutral grey easel and to report anything seen there.

To measure eidetic ability four coloured pictures were then exposed, one at a time for a period of 30 seconds. The subjects were then instructed to gaze naturally at a picture and to allow their eyes to look over it. When the 30 seconds exposure was complete each picture was removed and the subjects were asked to describe anything that they now saw on the easel. Subjects were then asked to answer specific questions and report when the image had faded if one had been obtained. Memory for details of a picture was tested again after an image had faded.

From each subject's taped report eight scores were obtained. These scores were based upon the presence or absence of *positive colour* reported to one or more of the eight stimulus cards; the *duration* of any images reported; the *accuracy* of *the colouring* of picture details; the *accuracy* of the answers given in response to each of the specific questions. Two judges scored the tape recorded report of each subject and obtained high indices of agreement.

The analysis enabled all the subjects to be placed into one or other of three categories as shown in Table 3.1. All subjects obtained after-images to one or more of the coloured squares but no subject was able to scan his after-images. No image at all was obtained by 67 subjects in response to the four pictures. Of the remaining 84 subjects who obtained an image of some kind to one or more of the pictures, only 12 obtained an image to each picture. These 12 subjects showed four other qualitative and quantitative differences from the other 72 subjects: first, they were the only ones to obtain an image to each picture which lasted for more than 40 seconds; second, their scores for detail were never less than 6 with the majority scoring 8 or 9 out of a possible 9; third, their images to all of the pictures could be scanned, unlike the usual after-image which moves with movements of the eye; fourth, of the forty-eight images seen by these 12 subjects, 90 % of them were positively coloured compared with only 34 % of the images obtained by the remaining 72 subjects.

A comparison of the three groups in relation to their responses to the coloured squares showed no difference between the 72 subjects with non-eidetic imagery and the 67 subjects who were completely imageless. When these 139 subjects were compared with the 12 eidetic subjects some further differences were found. The eidetic group obtained significantly more after-images to the squares, significantly more positive after-images and after-images which persisted for a significantly longer period.

When memory for picture details was measured after the eidetic-image had faded, the eidetic subjects recalled more than the members of the other two groups. However, this slight, though statistically significant superiority, might have been due to one or both of two possible factors. It might be due to the longer time that the eidetic subjects had available for inspecting the pictures (exposure time plus the time for which the image persisted). It might be due to the rehearsal of details while the eidetic subjects were describing their images.

When the 12 eidetic children and 40 of the others were retested eight months later, all 12 were still eidetic and only one of the others showed eidetic ability.

This study of the Havers' supports the view that eidetic imagery is a form of imagery relatively distinct from both after imagery and memory imagery, but it also emphasizes what should be obvious; that the incidence of eidetic ability in any population is dependent upon the criteria that are applied. Klüver (1931) reports that the incidence in non-adult populations has been variously estimated all the way from 0% to 100%. 'There seems to have been general agreement that EI range from "weak" to "strong", in other words, that there are "degrees" of eidetic imagery.' Obviously there is little meaning to any percentage unless the age and sex of the population is quoted along with the particular procedure used for eliciting eidetic-images and a statement of the criteria employed for determining whether or not an eidetic-image is present and to what degree.

When the same strict criteria used by the Habers are adopted somewhat similar percentages of eidetic ability are found in somewhat similar populations of children, despite the geographical and temporal distribution of the studies. See Table 3.1.

It is of historical interest to note that Galton (1880) found that 18 of his 172 Charterhouse boys (10%) reported the ability to project vivid stable images of what might now be called eidetic-images. For example, one of the boys said,

36

TABLE 3.1

Percentage of children giving eidetic, non-eidetic
and imageless responses in three studies of eidetic imagery

Type of Response	Teasdale (1934)		Morsh & Abbott (1945)		Haber & Haber (1964)	
	f	%	f	%	f	%
Eidetic imagery	11	6	24	9	12	8
Non-eidetic imagery	53	31	155	61	72	48
Imageless	109	63	77	30	67	44
Totals	173	100	256	100	151	100

'Holding a blank piece of paper in my hand, I can imagine on it a photograph or any object that it will hold.' The figure of 10% closely approximates those shown in Table 3.1.

Some cross-cultural studies using the Haber and Haber (1964) criteria have already appeared. Leonard Doob (1964, 1965) investigated eidetic imagery among the members of two non-literate societies in Africa; the Ibo of Eastern Nigeria and the Kamba of Central Kenya. Samples of children and adults from the Ibo and from the Kamba were tested. A total of 20% were found to be eidetic among the former and 13% among the latter. In subsequent investigations in other African societies Doob (1966) reports a total of 4% among the Masai, 0% among the Somali and 7% among the Swahili.

The Haber and Haber procedure was also used by Siipola and Hayden (1965) in their study of eidetic imagery among intellectually retarded children.

Because Jaensch believed that eidetic imagery is more common at lower age levels, many investigators have examined their data for age trends. Both Teasdale (1934) and Morsh and Abbott (1945) have shown this trend for unselected samples between the ages of 10 and 19 years. Teasdale found 12.5% with eidetic imagery in their eleventh year, 8.3% in their twelfth year, 5.8% in their thirteenth year reducing to only 2.1% among those in their fourteenth year. Of the few accounts that are available concerning eidetic imagery in adults (e.g. Bousfield and Barry, 1933) the report by Purdy (1936) is of special interest because his subject reported eidetic imagery in the modalities of sound, smell and touch in addition to sight. More recently Sheehan (1968) reported on an eidetic 21 year old, male, university student who gave colour responses to the monochomatic TAT pictures but who also appeared to possess vivid auditory imagery of an eidetic type. For example he said 'If you mention to me the first movements of Brahm's Fourth, I can actually hear it and I can hear the strings in perfect detail . . . '

Little reliable evidence exists for the relative incidence of eidetic imagery below the age of 10 years, and the problem of getting estimates at the pre-school level are especially great. Peck and Walling (1935) and Peck and Hodges (1937) recognized some of these difficulties but did not overcome them. For example, when number of details is taken as a main criterion, the 2 and 3 year old children are less likely to be classified as eidetic because their short attention span makes it less likely that they will continue observing the picture during the period of its exposure. The older child will not only have the advantage of a longer attention span but will also have a larger vocabulary with which to describe the details.

One of the partial solutions to the problem of testing young children may be to use procedures which minimize the need for verbal responses. An indication of a method worth further examination is provided by Klüver (1926). As part of a much larger study he required his subjects to look at a pair of black horizontal lines drawn parallel to one another on a piece of cardboard. On a separate piece of cardboard of the same size had been drawn a set of radiating lines as in the Hering illusion. The subjects were required to fixate the parallel lines for a period of 15 seconds, then the top card was removed while the subject continued to stare at the background of radiating lines. The expectation that the parallel lines would continue to be 'seen' and that they would now appear to be bowed outwards as in the normal Hering illusion, was fulfilled by only 3 of the 20 eidetic subjects employed in this experiment. A variety of other distortions were reported but Klüver believed that an implicit 'set of mind' to see the parallel lines in some unusual way was a more important determinant than the background lines. Though demand characteristics (Orne, 1962) may well play a part in experiments of this kind, the basic idea is a good one and should be developed further. For example, instead of asking the pre-school child or any other subject for a verbal report on this illusion he could be shown several comparison figures from which to select the one most like what he had seen.

Several other workers have exploited the possibility of combining an eidetic image with an objective stimulus. Gengerilli (1930) reports on a 15 year old girl with eidetic ability who was able to judge whether the diameter of an eidetically imaged circle was the same as, less than, or greater than, the length of any given stimulus square. Her accuracy was perfect and the task became a boring one. As she described her procedure she . . .

. . . put the circle on the square, and if the sides of the circle 'stick out' of the sides of the square the circle is too big; if the circle doesn't reach the sides of the square, it is too small. It's just like placing a real circle on top of a square.

In another study by Meenes (1933) 34 out of 100 negro school children were reported to be eidetic.

Most of these subjects succeeded in synthesizing a figure consisting of two parts, one of which formed an eidetic image which was projected upon a background containing the other. There was no phenomenological difference between the eidetic and non-eidetic part of the figure in the synthesis.

It is possible to improve the Meenes procedure by arranging that when the real and the imaged picture are superimposed, they form a new and unexpected composite. Something similar was tried by Siipola and Hayden (1965). Two pictures were scanned successively and over half of the eidetic subjects reported a composite image. None of the non-eidetic subjects reported this novel composite.

Functional Significance of eidetic imagery

The evidence available so far clearly indicates that a form of percept-like imagery exists in some children, in a few adolescents and in even fewer adults. It is more common in brain-injured retardates than in other retarded children. Among the two African tribes studies by Doob (1964, 1965) those who had least knowledge of English and/or least contact with Western culture were the ones most likely to possess eidetic imagery.

However, the evidence from the three other African societies (Doob, 1966) does not support any simple negative association between these indirect measures of abstract ability or of cognitive complexity and the possession of eidetic ability.

Nevertheless the trend of these observations still provides some support for the traditional view that eidetic imagery is part of a more general mode of concrete functioning which in the normally developing Western child disappears as he enters on his high school education. During the pre-adolescent period of physical and cerebral maturation the increased capacity for abstract thought is stimulated and encouraged in most school subjects. In accord with this trend, linguistic skills in oral and written expression take precedence over the inexpressible image. Though some personally experienced events may continue to be registered with something of their original sensory-affective quality, such events are also categorized in more abstract terms. Language is used more and more to compress, to represent and to express our experience. It is typically of more practical use for me to recall *that* I went to the post office yesterday and left a book on the counter when buying half-a-dozen four cent stamps, than it is to recall *what* the sensory-affective experience of being in the post office was actually like. To re-see re-hear and re-feel the experience is uneconomical. Under these conditions it is perhaps not so surprizing that the ability to use eidetic imagery in those who once possessed it begins to wither away from lack of use. Once lost it is not usually regained.

What functions, if any, does eidetic imagery serve before it atrophies? Why is it ever of utilitarian value, as opposed to aesthetic value, for perceptual experience to persist in memory relatively unchanged? Allport (1924) suggests that:

The EI seems to serve essentially the same purpose in the mental development of the child as does the repetition of a stimulus situation. It permits the 'concrete' sensory aspects of the surrounding world to penetrate thoroughly into his mind . . . Such pseudo-sensory experiences enables him to 'study out' in his own way and in his own time the various possibilities for response contained within the stimulus situation.

Jaensch (1930) believed that all young children are eidetic. This is probably not true though at the moment there is no satisfactory method of putting such a hypothesis to the test. At the age of 6 or 7, however, testing becomes more reliable. In what concommitant ways do those with and without eidetic imagery differ from one another? Are those who lose eidetic ability early in some way negatively reinforced by the significant others in their environment? Are those who retain it longest positively reinforced for having a rare gift? What in fact are the attitudes of parents towards eidetic children? Are parents ever aware that they have eidetic children? To what extent are eidetic children aware of their ability and to what extent and in what situations do they make a deliberate attempt to use it? Are eidetic children slower in their ability to form abstract concepts? Answers to these and many other questions are not yet available. But in relation to memory functioning, present evidence (Doob, 1965) indicates that eidetic imagery does not necessarily enable its possessor to recall the past more *accurately* but does appear to give greater *confidence* and greater *vividness* to recall.

This greater vividness showed itself in the way that: 'Details recalled in the present tense (immediately or weeks after the original exposure) have perhaps more "warmth" or "meaning" or they seem more "real" or "compelling" . . . than ones described as having been viewed in the past.'

In a study of the part played by imagery in learning, Jenkin (1935) reported that subjects were more confident when material was encoded in terms of imagery than when encoded in linguistic terms. That the greater confidence provided by imagery is no guarantee of recall accuracy is well illustrated by the girl in Jenkin's experiment who reported the most imagery and was the most confident of all the children in the study. This same little girl was the one most often wrong. Again, Bartlett (1932) concluded on the basis of his experiments on details remembered from picture postcards containing the faces of five members of the armed services, that the visual image 'is followed by an increase in confidence entirely out of proportion to any objective accuracy that is thereby secured.'

On the other hand the extraordinarily accurate eidetic memories shown by a few of Allport's (1924) subjects must not be forgotten. In what ways do children with consistently accurate eidetic memories differ from those whose eidetic memories are consistently less accurate?

In those who have been eidetikers when young, but who have

lost the ability at maturity is there any means by which it might be reinstated? Are there any conditions under which the non-eidetiker may manifest eidetic ability? Some evidence exists to suggest that the use of hallucinogenic drugs might be a valuable research strategy. Klüver (1926a, 1928a) has suggested many similarities between mescal visions and eidetic imagery, though he was unable to obtain eidetic-images in himself under conditions of mescalin intoxication. Jaensch (1930) has reported that non-eidetic individuals did produce eidetic-images after taking mescalin. He does not say whether the age of the subject was an important variable.

Chapter 4

MEMORY IMAGERY

MEMORY imagery is the common and relatively familiar imagery of everyday life. It may accompany the recall of events from the past, the ongoing thought processes of the present or the anticipatory actions and events of the future. Though it may occur as a spontaneous accompaniment to much everyday thought of this kind it is far more amenable to voluntary control than all other forms of imagery. However, the ability to control even this form of imagery varies very much from person to person and some of the consequences of this fact will be discussed at several places in this chapter.

Unlike the after-image, the eidetic-image or the imagination-image, there is seldom any likelihood that a memory-image could be mistaken for a genuine percept. Though in some few persons it may approach the vividness, clarity, colour, stability and duration of an eidetic-image it is typically more like a hazy etching, often incomplete and usually unstable, of brief duration and indefinitely localized.

Relatively unclear visual images of this kind have been found by Perky (1910) and Goldthwait (1933) to be associated with gross movements of the eyes. Similarly the memory-images of sounds and odours were found by Perky to be associated with movements of the larynx and the nostrils respectively. Wheeler (1928) believed that some peripheral activity was always present when imagery was evoked in any modality. He writes: 'It is much easier to image warm when the skin is warm or cold when the skin is cold. It may be doubted whether it is possible to have tactual imagery localized on an anaesthetic area.' Whether Wheeler is correct in this

43

latter assertion might be difficult to investigate satisfactorily, but the general view of peripheral involvement in memory imaging seems to have been a common one (e.g. Hicks, 1924). As suggested in the first chapter it may be that some degree of peripheral activity is present during all forms of imaging, but at the moment there is insufficient evidence for such a generalization.

In studies by Antrobus, Antrobus and Singer (1964) and by Singer and Antrobus (1965) eye movements as measured by the electrical oculargram (EOG) technique were found to be very slight during periods when visual images were reported. In contrast to this result it was found that when an ongoing daydream was actively suppressed, eye movements became much more frequent. Similar results were obtained, both with eyes open and with eyes closed. Slightly different results were obtained at another stage in the experiment when subjects were required to imagine particular scenes. When a subject with eyes closed was called on to imagine 'a man on a trampoline' a significant increase in vertical tracking eye movements occurred. When asked to imagine 'a tennis match' the tracking movements were more frequently in the horizontal plane. These tracking effects were less definite under the open eyes condition than in the eyes closed condition.

At this stage there is little to be gained from any further discussion of the attributes and concomitants of the memory-image. It may well be that the attributes of all forms of imagery vary on continua and are in no sense discrete. For the moment it is proposed to begin the discussion of this everyday form of concrete memory imagery by examining research related to its major dimensions of vividness and controllability. A contrast will then be made between those persons who habitually employ concrete memory imagery in their remembering and in their thinking and those who habitually employ the form of verbal imagery called inner speech. Though most people appear to have both modes of thought available to them, there is some evidence to suggest that a small number rely *almost* exclusively upon one or other mode. The chapter will conclude with a discussion of research findings and general speculations regarding the part played by memory-images in several other psychological processes.

Vividness of voluntary concrete imagery

In beginning with a discussion of imagery vividness it is important to bear in mind the distinction first made explicit by Griffitts (1927) that comparisions between individuals and comparisons within individuals should be kept separate. Inter-individual comparisons refer to the comparison between individuals either with reference to their total vividness of imagery scores or with reference to vividness scores on particular modalities. Intra-individual comparisons on the other hand, have reference to the relative vividness of imagery in one mode compared with the vividness of imagery in another mode as these occur in each individual. The same distinction would hold, of course, if comparisons on other dimensions of imagery are to be made.

1. Inter-individual comparisons

Most tests of vividness have been based upon the original questionnaire method introduced by Galton (1880) and criticized by Bain (1880). Of those that followed, the most important have almost certainly been the Betts (1909) test and the Sheehan shortened form of this test, developed at the University of Sydney (Sheehan, 1967). Peter Sheehan took 120 items from the original Betts test and administered them to a group of subjects. For the correlation between items within each of the seven modalities (visual, auditory, cutaneous, kinaesthetic, gustatory, olfactory and organic) a separate factor analysis was undertaken. In the final form of the revised test, 5 items were selected for each modality. When the total test of 35 items was used it was found that most of the variance could be accounted for by a single general factor of vividness. Even in Betts's (1909) investigation the high inter-modality correlations had suggested that a general factor of imagery vividness existed. When cross-validation samples were given both the original form of the Betts test and the 35-item revised form, correlations in excess of 0.90 were obtained for total vividness of imagery scores. In an unpublished study by the writer, 162 first year students from the University of Western Australia were given the shortened form of the Betts test as part of a battery containing six other cognitive tests. Administration was conducted with groups of between 30 and 40 students. Inter-correlations between scores on the seven modalities ranged from 0.44 for olfactory and visual, to 0.68 for tactile and audi-tory. Correlations between scores on individual modalities and total vividness scores ranged from 0.70 for visual to 0.83 for tactile. The 19 x 19 correlation matrix contained scores derived from the other six tests as well as vividness scores for each modality and a total vividness of imagery score. Separate correlation matrices were constructed for males and females and each was factor-analysed by the Householder method programmed for an IBM1620 computor (Moore and Ross, 1964). Nine factors were extracted and after varimax rotation all seven of the imagery subtests loaded the first factor. For the males the lowest rotated factor loading was 0.594 on the organic modality and the highest was 0.951 for total vividness of imagery. For the females the lowest loading was once again on the organic modality (0.718) and the highest 0.990 for total vividness of imagery. These independent replications provide some evidence for the purity of the short form of the Betts test, as a measure of overall imagery vividness (a copy of this test is provided in Appendix A). A test-retest reliability check pro-duced a correlation of 0.78 after a time interval of seven months (Sheehan, 1967b).

Some indication of the utility of this test has been provided by Sheehan himself (Sutcliffe, 1963, 1964; Sheehan, 1966b, 1967c) in a series of experiments in which some of the differen-tial consequences of possessing vivid and weak imagery have been investigated. The aim of the first experiment was to find out whether a previously perceived stimulus pattern could be reproduced more accurately under instructions to 'image' the original percept than under instructions to 'recall' it. Both groups were matched on the range of imagery vividness scores represented. Stimulus patterns of varying complexity were used, but it was always found that the reconstructions were more accurate under the 'image' condition than under 'recall'.

The investigator questioned whether this result represented a genuine cognitive difference, or whether it might not repre-sent no more than a difference in motivation. The instruction, 'to call to mind and retain an image—a mental picture in your mind's eye—of the design you saw on the screen a minute ago', may well contain a greater implicit request to retain accurate details than the instruction, 'to recall the pattern of the design you saw on the screen a minute ago'.

To check on this possibility another comparable sample of 30 subjects was used in which one sub-sample of 10 subjects received the same '*image*' instructions as before and two '*recall*' sub-samples were each given instructions which, in different ways, stressed accuracy of reproduction. Despite this emphasis upon accuracy in the 'recall' groups, the 'image' group was still found to be more accurate.

In both the preceding experiments the subjects in the 'image' condition were asked to rate the vividness of the imaged stimulus that they obtained. For this purpose the seven-step rating scale from the Betts test was used. An inverse relation between complexity of the stimuli and vividness of imaged stimuli was found. This finding supports the conclusions of other investigators (e.g., Slatter, 1960) who have reported that it is more difficult to obtain a vivid image of a complex stimulus pattern than it is to obtain a vivid image of a simple pattern.

When overall scores of vividness on the Sheehan test were examined in relation to accuracy of reproduction the plot of scores was found to be curvilinear. Though weak imagers might be accurate or inaccurate, those with vivid imagery were almost always more accurate. It should be noted that, when any subjective test of imaging ability is used, it is imperative that the subjects understand the difference between a vivid memory and a vivid memory image. It is possible to have vivid recall of what a house looks like, in the sense of *knowing* with certainty, how many windows face on to the front lawn, the shape of the chimney, the number of steps leading up to the front door, yet this may not involve a visual image of the house. If a subject confuses *vividness of knowing* with *vividness of picturing*, and *mutatis mutandis* for the other modalities, he may obtain a high score on the imagery test and be very accurate in the reproduction of a visual pattern, yet he may still have weak imagery.

Though in several of the studies conducted by the writer and reported in this volume group administration of imagery tests has been employed, he is now convinced that the only safe procedure is to administer these tests to individuals or small groups of four or five subjects after close discussion to ensure that the nature of memory imagery is understood.

In the very first of Sheehan's experiments mentioned above, subjects in an image condition control group were exposed to the stimulus patterns on two occasions instead of one and, as a result, it was found that this added familiarity with the stimuli led to higher ratings of vividness for the imaged stimuli. To examine this familiarity phenomenon further the effect of repeated presentation of a stimulus pattern upon the rated vividness of its image was investigated under 'image' instructions. The actual task of a subject in all these experiments is to construct a pattern with blocks from a stimulus pattern projected on to a screen. Then, after an interval occupied by the completion of another task, the subject attempts to reconstruct the original stimulus pattern either from an image or by recall. In the present experiment conducted under the 'image' condition this sequence was repeated ten times with the same stimulus. After each reconstruction trial was completed the subject was asked to rate the vividness of his image and the degree of confidence that he felt in the accuracy with which the imaged reconstruction matched the original stimulus pattern. Though improvement in performace over the ten trials was found to be the same for both the weak and the vivid imagers (based on scores on the short form of the Betts test), the vivid imagers showed a steady increase in the vividness of their imagery ratings with each increase in familiarity with the stimulus. In contrast with these findings the ratings made by the weak imagers, of their imaged stimulus patterns, remained throughout at a uniformly low level of vividness. Sheehan concludes: 'Once a poor imager, always a poor imager; but for those who have them images can become more vivid with increasing familiarity with their stimulus objects.'

In a second series of experiments designed, like the first, to investigate the relation between vividness of imagery and accuracy of recall Sheehan (Sutcliffe, 1964; Sheehan, 1966a) employed an entirely different task. An apparatus was constructed which enabled the brightness, clarity and size of a simple geometric design to be varied. The geometric designs were projected on to the back of a milkglass screen according to predetermined settings on each of the three stimulus variables. The subject viewed a stimulus for 10 seconds, then closed his eyes while the stimulus was removed. He was then given 35 seconds in which to produce and hold a memory-image of the stimulus, at the end of which time he opens his eyes and adjusts the controls so that the stimulus pattern matches the memory image of the original stimulus. As in the first series of experiments, the vividness of each memory image was rated on a seven step scale. When the subject had set the three controls, the readings were recorded by the experimenter and each compared with the settings used when projecting the original stimulus. In this way accurate measures could be obtained of the similarities and differences between the imaged stimulus and the perceptual stimulus. As in the first series of experiments, subjects who were vivid imagers tended to be uniformly accurate, while subjects who were weak imagers showed a wide spread from the highly accurate to the highly inaccurate.

Clearly the absence of vivid visual imagery does not preclude the possibility of accurate perceptual memories, but it is of some importance that the possession of vivid imagery may significantly increase the chances of being accurate.

2. *Intra-individual comparisons*

A slightly different approach to the measurement of vividness was adopted by Griffitts (1927) in his clearness of concrete imagery test, which provides for each individual an indication of his hierarchy of imagery vividness. Though some subjects found the task rather difficult, test retest reliabilities were obtained of 0.85 (visual), 0.72 (auditory) and 0.79 (kinaesthetic). Test retest intervals ranged between one and eight weeks for the 43 psychology student subjects involved.

The test consists of 130 objects to be imaged. Against the name of each object is the type of image to be produced. Thus, Item 128 is shown as 'Tac. Sandpaper' which indicates to the subject that a tactile image of sandpaper is to be obtained and no other. Before beginning the test the subject is required to look through the entire list and select five objects, irrespective of modality, which can be imaged more clearly than any others in this list. These serve as standards and are immediately given the highest possible rating of 10. All other objects are to be rated for vividness against these standards on a 0—10 rating scale.

Results were obtained for 87 subjects, of whom 90 % had

images of the greatest clarity or vividness in the visual mode, 5 % in the auditory and 5 % in the kinaesthetic modes.

In 76% of those cases where visual ranks first, auditory ranks second; in 24% kinaesthetic ranks second. In every case where auditory ranks first, visual is a close second. In the 5 cases where kinaesthetic ranks first, visual is second in 3 and auditory in 2.

As this test takes each individual as his own standard, conclusions can only be drawn in terms of the rank order of his imagery vividness in the different modalities tested. Though twenty people might have the same rank order (e.g., visual, auditory, kinaesthetic) the vividness of visual imagery in one of them might be almost perceptlike, while in another it might be relatively indistinct and blurred.

Controllability of voluntary concrete imagery

From at least the time of Galton (1883) the dimension of controllability has had a place in the discussion of mental imagery. Jaensch (1930) made it the basis of a personality typology which in turn was supposedly related to differences in the eidetic imagery that each experienced. The B (Basedowoid) type was believed to have eidetic-images which were under voluntary control and more like memory-images, while at the other extreme the T (Tetanoid) type was said to have eidetic-images which come and go and change with the independence of an after-image.

As part of a study on factors associated with the formation of national stereotypes, Rosemary Gordon (1949) developed a test of imagery control in which a 'Yes' or 'No' answer was required to each of the following questions:

> *Can you see a car standing in front of a garden gate? What is its colour? Try and see it in a different colour.*
> *Can you now see the same car lying upside down?*
> *Now put the same car back on its four wheels.*
> *Now can you see the car running along the road?*
> *Can you see it climb up a very steep hill?*
> *Can you see it climb across the top?*
> *Can you see it get out of control and crash through a house?*
> *Can you now see the same car running along the road with a handsome couple inside?*

Now can you see the car cross a bridge and fall over the side into the
   stream below?
Can you now see the car all old and dismantled in a car cemetery?

This test was administered to a total of 118 subjects all but 1 of
whom had visual imagery. When everyone of the test scenes
was answered 'Yes', the subject was categorized as 'controlled';
when one or more scenes was answered 'No', the subject was
categorized as 'autonomous'. Altogether there were 74 'controlled' and 40 'autonomous' students. Four subjects were
excluded from the analysis. It was found that the possession of
'autonomous' (uncontrolled) imagery was associated with the
evocation of conventional stereotyped imagery to the nation
stimulus words (Englishman, Chinese, German, Jew) and that
these images were associated with experiences that had
occurred earlier in life than the less stereotyped images of the
'controlled imagery' (autonomous) subjects.

   In a subsequent study, Gordon (1950) found that of a sample
of 42 male neurotic patients who took this test, 20 possessed
'autonomous' imagery and 22 'controlled' imagery. She predicted that the 'controlled' subjects should be able to exert
more influence on the reversal rate of a Necker cube than
'autonomous' subjects. Normal rates of reversal for the two
groups were approximately the same—10.05 fluctuation per
minute for the autonomous group compared with 10.64 for the
controlled group. Group means for the fast and slow speeds
were in the predicted directions but were not significantly
different. However, if control over rate of reversal was scored
on an individual basis, as the *difference* between normal and fast
rates, then a significant difference in the predicted direction
was found. Similarly, a significant difference between the two
groups was obtained if individual scores based upon the
difference between rate of reversal under fast and under slow
conditions was used.

   This relationship between control over the behaviour of a
percept and control over the behaviour of an image is further
supported from data published by Costello (1956, 1957). For
example, in the 1957 study Costello showed that psychiatrically
diagnosed groups of dysthymics and hysterics both had
relatively uncontrolled imagery when compared with a control
group of normals. The dysthymics had vivid uncontrolled

imagery, the hysterics weak unstable (uncontrolled) imagery, whilst the normals had either weak or vivid controlled imagery. Among the tentative conclusions of this study was the suggestion that 'type of imagery indicates more the type of disorder to which the individual may be prone rather than indicating mental disorder itself.' If this were true then it might be expected that an analysis of imaging abilities in relation to Eysenck's (1953) personality dimensions should reveal the same results with a sample of normal subjects. Eysenck (1957) defines the dysthymic as an introverted neurotic and the hysteric as an extraverted neurotic. It was predicted, therefore, that introverted neurotics, extroverted neurotics and a combined group of extroverted and introverted normals would have respectively: vivid uncontrolled imagery, weak uncontrolled imagery and controlled imagery that might be either weak or strong. Two unpublished investigations of this hypothesis (Richardson, 1962) employing the short form of the M.P.I. test of introversion-extroversion, the short form of the Betts test of imagery vividness, and the Gordon test of imagery control, provided some support for the prediction. However, in two more recent attempts at replication using larger samples and the long form of the M.P.I. the differences were not significant. Controlled visualizers showed a consistent tendency throughout all four studies to be normals (i.e., either introvert or extrovert but non-neurotic), but in the two more recent studies no association between type of neuroticism and type of uncontrolled imagery was found.

Before ending this discussion on controllability of voluntarily evoked concrete images, it is worth noting the similarity between what has been described as an autonomous image by Gordon and the characteristics of some of the imagination images to be discussed in the next chapter. For example, McKellar (1957) points out that *autonomy* is the 'fundamental and central attribute of hypnagogic imaging'. This spontaneous and uncontrolled quality seems to be common among other less dramatic forms of imagination imagery. For example, some of the subjects who reported imagination images in Griffitts' (1927) test of clearness and stability of visual imagery, found it difficult to control them. One subject had imaged a circle and reported, 'The circle, just out in space, is always turning rapidly in spite of all I can do to hold it still. I try to hold it in place but it finally gets away from me and rolls off to the left. When I get it back it does the same thing again.'

Vividness and controllability of voluntary concrete imagery in relation to visualizing efficiency

The part played by visual imagery in tests of spatial or visualizing ability is unclear. It may turn out to be quite irrelevant but it is more probable that visual imagery will be found to have some limited value. Perhaps, as Peter Sheehan found in the research reviewed earlier in this chapter, the vivid visual imager almost always does well on recalling spatial tasks of some kinds whereas the weak visual imager may or may not do well. Be this as it may, there is more to solving a spatial task than the ability to have vivid visual images, and for this reason the term 'visualizing efficiency', first proposed by Griffitts (1927), seems to be a more appropriate one than 'visualizing ability'. Nevertheless, there is evidence that visualizing efficiency depends very much on genetic endowment. Thurstone (1951) reports a factor analytic study based upon the scores obtained by 150 pairs of identical and fraternal twins on 40 different group and individual tests. The results showed that identical twins were more alike on these tests than were the fraternal twins and that this association was expecially marked on the tests defining the visualizing factor.

Griffitts' own test of visualizing efficiency consisted of a series of sixteen problems involving the spatial manipulation of two-and three-dimensional figures and the solution of such problems as the following: 'My house faces the street. If a boy passes by my house in the morning walking towards the rising sun, with my house at his right, which direction does my house face?' Five minutes were allowed for the solution of each problem. The overall score for this test was based upon the total time taken, in seconds, for all sixteen problems. Problems which were unsolved at the end of 5 minutes were counted as 400 seconds. A reliability co-efficient of 0.72 was obtained between scores on the first twelve problems and scores on the last four (N =43). Correlations between scores on this test and scores on the visual imagery components of Griffits' tests of dominance and vividness were low but positive:

E   53

Visualization x Dominance $r = 0.12$
Visualization x Vividness $r = 0.27$
Dominance x Vividness $r = 0.58$

'Subjects who failed with any problem *always* attributed their failure to an inability to picture the figure in their mind, or to hold the image long enough to count the parts, and this without any suggestions from the experimenter.'

A few years later El Koussy (1935) reported that his subjects frequently said that they used visual imagery in solving spatial tasks, but more recent research suggests that visual imaging skills may be necessary in some but not all such tasks. Unfortunately, the evidence is not conclusive as to which subclass of spatial task is more likely to require visual imagery, but that subclasses exist has been conclusively demonstrated from well-replicated factor analytic studies.

The first review of these studies was produced by Michael (1949) who reported several investigators as having shown two factors to be present on two slightly different kinds of spatial test. One of these factors was called spatial orientation (S) and the other visualization (VZ). Improved tests for the measurement of each of these factors have been reported by French and his colleagues (1963). The difference between the two subclasses is said to be in terms of the reference axis used by the subject. In spatial orientation tests, the subject uses right-left, top-bottom and front-back in relation to his own body. His task is to recognize whether the spatial relations of one pattern are similar or different to those of another. Thurstone's Cube test and his Flag test are among those that define this factor.

In contrast to the spatial orientation factor, the visualization factor loads those tests that require a subject 'to move, rotate, turn, twist, or invert one or more objects'. Two tests with high loadings on this factor are the Form Board test and the Punched Holes test of Thurstone. This latter test requires the subject to look at a symbolic representation of a folded sheet of paper which has had one or more holes punched in it. The task is to select the example which shows what the paper will look like when it has been unfolded. As opposed to an ability to recognize the essential similarity of two spatial patterns, these visualization tasks involve the slightly more complex ability to manipulate mentally the elements of a spatial pattern. It is sometimes assumed that visualization as here defined involves the use of visual imagery to a greater extent than spatial orientation tasks, which can perhaps be solved by a process of reasoning without any visual representation occurring.

However, this convenient conclusion is not supported in a study by Barratt (1953). He factor-analysed the scores on twenty-three spatial medium tests of approximately 50 undergraduates and obtained three factors: (i) Spatial manipulation; (ii) Spatial reasoning; (iii) Shape recognition. These three factors were later confirmed on a sample of 180 secondary school boys. The twelve tests which best defined these factors were administered to a further sample of subjects who were asked to rate the vividness of the visual imagery that had been spontaneously aroused while solving each of them. It was found that those who had the most vivid imagery aroused on the Cube test and the Flag test did significantly better than those whose spontaneous imagery was relatively weak. These two tests defined Barratt's spatial manipulation factor; tests which in the French battery define spatial orientation and not visualization. The second factor of spatial reasoning was defined by such tests as the Raven's Progressive Matrices. Factor three was concerned with shape recognition and was defined most clearly by a form board test. Though imagery played some part in successful performances on tests loading this third factor, and none on tests loading the second factor of spatial reasoning, it was with tests on the so-called spatial manipulation factor that vivid spontaneous imagery was most clearly associated.

Is vividness of imagery of greater value on visualization tests as Michael (1949) has suggested, or is it of greater value on tests of spatial orientation (manipulation) as is suggested by the results of Barratt's (1953) investigations or is visual imagery equally relevant or irrelevant to both? Is the apparent contradiction between Barratt and Michael due to a difference between the presence of *spontaneous* visual imagery on the one hand, and the ability to produce visual imagery *voluntarily* when needed, on the other?

Whatever the part played by vividness in visualizing efficiency, there has been relatively little interest in the variable of imagery control. However, a beginning has been made by Costello (1956). He reports that when fifteen normal subjects were divided into a controlled and an uncontrolled (autonomous) group on the basis of Gordon's (1949) test, those with controlled imagery performed significantly better than those with uncontrolled imagery on the spatial test NIIP, Group Test 80A. No significant differences were found between the two groups on the Raven's Progressive Matrices, or on the Mill Hill vocabulary scale. Though no tests of imagery control were administered to his 12 patient subjects, Costello suggests that those . . .

. . . who before leucotomy scored low on the space tests had vivid autonomous imagery which was made weaker and more controlled by the operations, thus resulting in a higher post-operative score. Secondly, patients who had high scores before the operation had weak controlled imagery which was made weaker by the operation. The drop in score for these patients is apparently due to the fact that though their imagery is controllable, it is now too weak for the images to be formed easily.

The interaction of vividness and controllability in the utilization of voluntary concrete imagery

In this section a sample study concerned with mental practice will be presented, to show the way in which the two variables of vividness and controllability may interact to produce predictable differences in performance.

Mental practice may be defined as the symbolic rehearsal of a physical activity in the absence of any gross muscular movements. When a high jumper is waiting for his turn to jump and in imagination 'sees' and 'feels' himself going through the run up, take off, roll over and landing he is engaged in mental practice. A recent review of the literature by Richardson (1967a, 1967b) concluded that improved performance can result from this form of practice and that visual and kinaesthetic imaging abilities may well play a significant role in the amount of gain obtained by any particular individual.

The part played by imagery in accounting for individual differences in the amount of improvement that occurs under mental practice conditions has been suggested by several research workers. For example, Clark (1960) obtained reports from his subjects on their use of imagery during mental practice of a basketball skill which suggested that both the vividness and controllability of imagery might be important.

That vividness of imagery, if it is uncontrollable, may be more of a hindrance than a help is suggested by the observation of one subject who 'reported mentally attempting to bounce the ball preparatory to shooting only to imagine that it would not bounce and stuck to the floor. This disturbed him to a point where he could not successfully visualize the shooting technique.'

At the other extreme it might be expected that vivid controllable imagery would facilitate the process of mental practice and lead to larger gains in the performance of whatever motor skill might be involved.

In a first attempt to study this problem (Richardson and Start, 1963; Start and Richardson, 1964) an investigation was made into the effect of four combinations of vividness and controllability of imagery on level of skill attained in performing the single-leg upstart on the Olympic high bar. Specifically it was hypothesized that mental practice of this simple gymnastic skill would result in the highest levels of performance in those subjects who possessed *vivid controllable imagery* (VCI) followed by somewhat lower levels of performance in subjects having *weak controllable imagery* (W.C.I.); a lower level still was predicted for those who had *weak uncontrollable imagery* (WUI) and the lowest level of all in those subjects who possessed *vivid uncontrollable imagery* (VUI).

The subjects in this experiment were thirty-one second-year male trainee teachers aged 18 to 20 years. They were all brought together during a normal work period and the task and method explained to them. A brief questionnaire was administered to obtain information on age and athletic or sporting interests and activities. Practice periods lasted for five minutes on each of six days and were conducted using standardized instructions in which subjects were required to 'see' and 'feel' themselves through each of the movements described. None of the subjects had had any previous experience in the use of the high bar, though all but one observed a practical demonstration of the skill to be learned. Mental practice sessions took place in a bare lecture room with five or six subjects practising at one time.

On the day after the last mental practice, subjects were rated individually on their actual physical performance in mounting the high bar and the best of three attempts was taken as the final measure of performance. The ratings were made by

57

four independent judges all of whom were familiar with this skill as a result of their experience in judging competitive gymnastics. Inter-correlations between the ratings of the four judges ranged from 0.92 to 0.96.

In the fortnight following the completion of this part of the investigation the subjects were recalled and given an extensive test battery. To check on alternative hypotheses to the one-under test, correlations were calculated between the rank order of the thirty-one subjects on the gymnastic skill and the rank order of their scores on each of the following tests: Brace test of motor ability, measures of shoulder and hip strength, height, weight and intelligence. None of these correlations was significant and no systematic differences in sporting or athletic interests were found.

To obtain measures of imagery vividness and of control, the short form of the Betts test and a slightly modified version of the Gordon test (see Appendix B) were administered. As earlier work by Jacobson (1932) on the relation of imaging to muscle action currents, and by Arnold (1946) on the relation of imaging to body sway, both showed that a combination of visual and kinaesthetic imagery was more effective than visual alone, vividness scores based upon this combination were used.

To test the hypothesis, subjects scoring above and below the median on the Gordon test of imagery control were each subdivided at the median into a vivid and a weak imagery group. The mean performance scores (T scores) of the four imagery groups were as predicted: VCI (Mn.57.10)>WCI(Mn.51.88) >WUI(Mn.47.89)>VUI(Mn.47.36). The Mann-Whitney U test applied to a comparison of scores in the extreme groups indicated that they were significantly different (p.<.05; one tailed). Though the results are consistent with the hypothesis the design does not exclude the possibility of an alternative hypothesis. A crucial and difficult problem in studies of this kind is to ensure equality of motivation. If motivation differs between the four groups, difference in performance scores might be due to this factor rather than the cognitive factor of imagery. By not selecting groups until performance scores had been obtained it was possible to rule out the influence of competitive attitudes between groups. Data from post-experimental interviews suggested that interest in the project was fairly high among all participants. However, it is still possible that those who were successfully imaging the task during the mental practice periods maintained or increased their interest in performing well on the task, while those who found the mental practice difficult suffered a corresponding drop in motivation to perform well.

Dominance of spontaneous concrete imagery

The dominance of spontaneous concrete imagery refers to the modality hierarchy which exists for most persons who experience imagery as a spontaneous accompaniment to at least some of their remembering and thinking activities. Vividness of imagery is not the dimension of interest, but merely the frequency with which images tend to arise spontaneously in the different modalities.

After outlining the most common way of measuring the dominance of spontaneous concrete imagery, the results of two studies that have utilized this aspect of imagery will be described.

1. *Measurement*

A typical test of imagery dominance involves the auditory or visual presentation of a list of words, each of which refers to a familiar experience and which at the same time has the potentiality of arousing imagery in more than one modality. In the Griffitts (1927) test of imagery dominance, 75 words and 40 sentences were selected on the basis of these criteria. In a more recent study by Diehl and England (1958), a selection of only 20 words were used—13 from the Griffitts list: *telephone, bicycle, piano, fire, electric fan, hammer, tennis, clock, whistle, scissors, music, steam, fire engine*—and 7 from a list prepared by Robbins and Robbins (1948): *typewriter, car, ball, lawnmower, bell, gun, radio*. These were pretested as before and each word was found to elicit imagery in the three major modalities of vision, hearing and kinaesthesia.

The instructions to the subject in the Griffitts (1927) version of this test are as follows:

During this test please assume as much as possible the attitude of a passive spectator to what goes on in your mind. I will read a word from this list, and I want you to tell me just what comes into your mind as you think of the object. If it be the way it looks, answer

59

'visual'; if some sound, answer 'auditory'; if some muscular activity on your own part answer 'motor'; if it be a taste or smell, or heat or cold, answer accordingly. Don't try to get any particular kind of response, but let come what may. Please try to avoid the expression 'I thought of' or 'I thought about'.

A few words from a practice list were then presented. When one of those words had elicited more than one kind of imagery, the subject was asked, 'Which of the two (or three) seemed to be more dominant, that is, which is more in the centre of consciousness, and which more in the background?' When the subject had answered, he was told, 'I want to know not only which is the more dominant, but how much so. Out of a total of 7 points how many would you give to one and how many to the other?'

The scoring for the relative dominance of each modality was obtained by totalling the points for each modality and expressing them as a percentage of the total number of points. For example, in a 20-item test the total possible points for allocation would be 140. If 100 points had been given to the visual aspect of the evoked imagery and 20 points each to the auditory and motor aspects, the final score would be: V. 71.0; A. 14.5; K. 14.5.

In the Griffitts (1927) test, results for words and sentences were computed separately and the scores correlated. Reliability as measured in this way produced correlations of 0.83 for visual, 0.69 for auditory and 0.68 for the kinaesthetic mode. In another reliability study a subgroup of forty-three psychology students responded to the first 25 words of the 75-item list under conditions of visual presentation. Test retest reliability with one week interval was: for visual 0.83; for auditory 0.73; and for kinaesthetic 0.89. As might be expected the visual mode is dominant for the great majority of people.

2. *Applications*

Of the two applications of the type of measure just described the first is concerned with the dominance of imagery in blind and sighted adolescents, and the second with the dominant modality in which imagery occurs among students in different university faculties.

(a) Blind and sighted adolescents: At least as early as 1838 the observation had been made (Heermann, cited by Schlaegel (1953)) that visual dreams are seldom if ever experienced in persons who become totally blind before their seventh year. Schlaegel (1953) set out to investigate a comparable problem. What effect does degree of blindness and age of onset have upon the dominant mode of concrete imagery? A slightly modified form of the Griffitts test was administered to 67 students from the Indiana School for the Blind and to a roughly comparable group of 78 normally sighted Indianapolis high school students. Not all of the blind school students were totally blind. When the average imagery scores of the blind school and high school students were considered as a whole, the hierarchy of dominance was found to be the same for both—in the order: visual, auditory, kinaesthetic, tactile-temperature and olfactory-gustatory.

Of the 23 totally blind students, 16 had a dominance of auditory imagery compared with 9 out of the 44 partially blind and none of the sighted students. None of the 13 students who had become totally blind before the age of six had visual imagery dominant and only 3 of them had any visual imagery at all.

In writing about the problems of a person 'with profound deafness from early life' Myklebust (1964) suggests that such a person may become 'highly dependent on imagery, especially visual imagery, which may be a predominant factor in the restriction imposed on his psychological development as well as in the concreteness which results.'

(b) Imagery dominance in relation to undergraduate major subject: Diehl and England (1958) administered the twenty words listed earlier in this section to student samples majoring in art, physical education and music, and to a control group from the general student population. It was found that the mean dominance score for visual imagery was higher for art majors than for the control group. The kinaesthetic, or motor imagery, of the physical education majors had a mean dominance score higher than the control group, but no evidence of any difference on the mean dominance of auditory imagery was found when music majors were compared with the control.

Habitual modes of voluntary and spontaneous imaging

There has been a persistent trend in the literature on memory imagery to produce some viable typology which could be used for the classification of any population of interest to the investigator. The notion of pure imagery types based on modality was very popular around the turn of the century, but in careful introspective studies such as those made by Fernald (1912) or Betts (1909) pure visiles, audiles or motiles were never found. In the light of such studies as those of Sheehan (1967) which have shown high inter-modality correlations for vividness of imagery, the case for a typology based on modality is convincingly destroyed. Such findings do not mean, of course, that no individual exists who is entirely dependent upon a single imagery mode; it only means that such individuals are sufficiently rare to make a typology impossible.

An alternative typology which is probably as old as the other and is clearly related to it, will be examined in this section. This typology, or convenient classification, is based upon the observation that some people who have fairly vivid concrete imagery are *habitual visualizers*, while others who have relatively weak concrete imagery and little if any visual imagery are *habitual verbalizers* with a predominance of kinaesthetic imagery (sensation) from the larynx and tongue, and some verbal auditory imagery.

Writing on the visualizer and the vocalizer as he discovered them in the process of carrying out his memory experiments Bartlett (1932) noted that:

The person who, in *The Method of Description*, relied upon visual cues tended to do the same in *The Methods of Repeated Reproduction* and of *Picture Writing*. The subject who depended largely upon verbal descriptions and vocalization in the case of one experimental method did the same when the method of experiment was changed. The ways in which we deal with the various problems that confront us are, in fact, much less varied than the problems themselves.

In a moment of cheerful confidence Grey Walter (1953) estimated the incidence in an unselected population as 15 % each for habitual visualizers and habitual verbalizers with the remaining 70 % being able to switch backwards and forwards from visualizing to verbalizing whenever the nature of the task or personal preference demanded it. As with all the other estimates of imagery incidence discussed in this book its significance must necessarily depend upon the methods used for arriving at it. In the present instance the two basic methods that have been used involve measures of alpha blocking and breathing patterns.

After discussion of these neurological and physiological methods the section will be concluded with an account of habitual modes of voluntary and spontaneous imaging based upon subjective report.

1. *Classification based upon the alpha rhythm*

The classic study which inaugurated a completely new approach to imagery measurement was conducted by Golla, Hutton and Grey Walter (1943). They began by administering seven brief tests to each of their subjects. These tests included mental arithmetic, thinking over a story, recalling an event and repeating the Lord's Prayer to themselves. Subjects were questioned on how they had gone about these tasks and on the basis of the answers they were allocated to one or other of four groups: the visualizers in whom visual imagery predominated to the exclusion of almost all other modes; the verbalizers, whose imagery was almost exclusively auditory-kinaesthetic; and two mixed groups, distinguished on the basis of how closely they resembled the two extremes. The authors then proposed as a 'working hypothesis' that resting alpha-rhythm records could be classified into three groups and that the subjectively based imagery classification already established might be expected to show some correspondence to the alpha types.

The feature of the alpha rhythm selected as a basis of classification was its amplitude. The M or minus type was defined as having an alpha amplitude that did not exceed 10 microvolts with eyes closed. Being so low to begin with there was relatively little change when the eyes were opened, or when mental work was undertaken with eyes closed. It was believed that the M type of alpha was characteristic of the habitual visualizer.

In the P, or persistent type, an alpha amplititude of between 10 and 50 microvolts with eyes closed was found to persist when the eyes were opened, and when mental tasks were undertaken with eyes closed. This P type was thought to be typical of the habitual verbalizer. Finally, the R, or responsive type, which is the most common, is defined as one in which a normal resting alpha amplitude of 10—50 microvolts is obtained with eyes closed, but this relatively high voltage disappears or is considerably reduced when the eyes are opened. This common R type of alpha was equated with the mixed imagery category. The results of this study are shown in Table 4.1 below.

TABLE 4.1

Habitual imagery modes and related alpha types

Alpha Classification	Pure Visualizer	Mixed		Pure Verbalizer
		IMAGERY CLASSIFICATION		
		Predominantly Visual Some Aud/Kin	Predominantly Aud/Kin Some Visual	
M	13	9	–	–
R	–	12	15	–
P	–	3	6	2
Totals f	13	24	21	2
Totals %	22	40	35	3

A replication of this study conducted by Short (1953) on a patient sample (n=75) and on a normal sample (n=75) appeared to confirm these results and in addition found corresponding respiratory changes in the visualizers and the verbalizers. The visualizing M types tended to be regular breathers when solving problems whereas the verbalizing P types tended to be irregular breathers. He also observed that alpha rhythms tended to block when visual imagery was reported and to persist when verbal-motor imagery was used.

In a further investigation, Short and Walter (1954) found that M, R and P alpha classification was related to performance on a task in which differently grooved cement blocks were fingered by the subject from behind a screen and a report then given on the shape of each groove. Though Short (1953) had suggested that individuals of the R type 'are the most favoured in so far as they can readily adapt their models for different types of mental problems', the opposite finding was obtained with the stereognosis tasks used in the Short and Walter (1954) study. Both the habitual visualizers (M) and the habitual verbalizers (P) were superior in their performance to the mixed (R) type, who appeared to vacilate between the two modes 'as indicated by frequent and irregular bursts of alpha rhythm'. Perhaps the nature of the task determines whether a single habitual mode is superior, or inferior, to the more versatile mixed mode.

These studies by Grey Walter and his associates at the Burden Neurological Institute in Bristol did not go unchallenged and several more recent investigations by other workers in Britain and America must now be discussed.

Because other investigators have found difficulty in finding subjects whose resting alpha characteristics enabled them to be classified as M, R or P types, the relation of alpha blocking to reports of visual imagery, or performance on tasks believed to require visual imagery, has been examined. Barratt (1956) argued that if alpha blocking (suppression) is a reliable objective indicator of visual imaging then it should occur *only* under conditions of visualizing. To test this hypothesis, he administered a verbal reasoning problem and figure construction task to a volunteer sample of 51 normal males. His results showed that some alpha suppression occurred during the solution of both problems, but that significantly more suppression occurred during the visual problem than during the verbal problem. All subjects reported the use of visual imagery in the solution of the figure construction task, but only 10 reported any visual images while solving the verbal reasoning task. It was found that more suppression occurred for this subsample of 10 on the visual problem than occurred with the remaining 41 subjects on this problem. However, the fact that significant suppression effects occurred among those who utilized visual imagery least, led Barratt to the conclusion that: 'there is little to support an argument for alpha-amplitude loss as an objective measure of visual imagery'. He then goes on to state that:

All the evidence so far educed from the statistical data and verbal reports indicates that although image-provoking problem situations reduce the amplitude of the alpha rhythm, the converse proposition that amplitude reduction is a measure of visual imaging is not confirmed. Amplitude reduction is associated with visual imagery and with a number of other conditions as well.

Though this study has usually been interpreted as providing results opposed to the visual imagery alpha-suppression hypothesis, it should of course be regarded at the worst as neutral on this issue. The fact that coughing will produce a GSR response does not invalidate it as a measure of arousal level. The fact that an increase in mental effort (attention, alertness) produces some decrease in alpha amplitude does not in itself deny the value of alpha blocking as a measure of visualizing providing that it is possible to control all these other conditions suspected of reducing alpha amplitude. It is clear that Barratt is aware of this when he writes that a measure is adequate if 'the particular conditions under which it does operate as an indicator should be precisely specified'.

Using two verbal and two non-verbal questions Stewart and MacFarlane Smith (1959) confirmed Barratt's (1956) finding that both types of question produced some alpha suppression, but significantly more suppression occurred while answering the 'visual' type questions. When the records were reclassified into the M, R and P types, no significant differences were found in the mean performance scores of these groups on the NIIP Memory for Design test, NFER Spatial Test I and the NFER Non Verbal Test 3, nor on the Moray House Adult Intelligence Test I. It would have been of interest to know how well each of these three alpha types had succeeded on the two visual and the two verbal questions administered concurrently with the EEG recordings. These questions are easier and may have produced supporting evidence for the alpha classification when no such evidence was available from the four written tasks which may have required more mental effort for their solution.

That voluntary imagery can be used most effectively when the task is relatively easy, rather than relatively hard, was noted earlier in discussing the experiments of Sheehan (Sutcliffe, 1962, 1963, 1964). Similar results have been reported by Costello and McGregor (1957) and by Slatter (1960) using EEG measures of imaging abilities. When a task is difficult then suppression may occur as a result of greater activation, quite apart from any imaging that might be involved. In fact a verbalizer who has to solve a visual type problem may have to exert himself much more than a visualizer. Both would then have low amplitude alpha, but for the visualizer this might be largely due to visual imagery, while for the verbalizer it might be largely due to greater arousal level.

Oswald (1957) goes somewhat further in his analysis of the confounding variable of 'arousal'. He puts forward the accepted view (Betts, 1909; Fox, 1915) that we are most likely to become aware of spontaneous imagery at those points in our thinking where some difficulty is met, where the solution to a problem fails to come. As alpha suppression is also associated with 'difficulty' and with the mental effort that this necessitates he goes on to propose: 'that suppression of the alpha rhythm may be explicable solely in terms of mechanisms controlling alertness, without reference to visual imagery.' His own study of 100 patients failed to show any significant association between M, R and P types of alph record and the regular/irregular breathing record dichotomy.

That the non-specific effects of any stimulation may influence arousal level and in turn produce varying degrees of alpha blocking has become a crucial problem in this area of research (e.g., Costello and McGregor, 1957; Drewes, 1958). Only in the study by Kamiya and Zeitlin (1963) is there clear evidence that the alpha suppression could be voluntarily controlled by a subject when he had learned that the controlling stimulus was his own visual imagery. Though alpha suppression occurred when the subject turned on his visual imagery, there were no changes in any other of the concommitant measures of arousal employed. It is of interest that the subjects in this experiment were not being required to exert great intellectual effort in the attempt to solve 'g' saturated spatial tasks. Perhaps it is on those tasks where visual imagery is spontaneous or relatively easy to produce that the clearest relation between alpha suppression and habitual imagery modes is most likely to be found. For example, Slatter (1960) used similar series of tasks to those of Golla, Hutton and Walter (1943) plus a brief test of voluntary imagery in which the subject looked at a picture for 20 seconds, closed his eyes and then after a lapse of 30 seconds tried to visualize the picture to himself. Of the 412 tasks undertaken by the 60 students in his sample, Slatter found a close correspondence between habitual mode of imaging (based on imagery reported by subjects when completing the series of tasks) and alpha suppression or persistence.

TABLE 4.2

*Slatter's (1960) results relating number of tasks
associated with different imagery and alpha characteristics*

Total No. of tasks	Visual imagery and Alpha suppression	Visual imagery and Alpha persistence	Verbal imagery and Alpha suppression	Verbal imagery and Alpha persistence
412	249	15	24	124

It appears from Table 4.2 that only 39 misclassifications have occurred out of a possible 412.

In the next study to be discussed, confounding between the two variables of visual imagery and mental effort or arousal may have occurred, but the study has several novel features which justifies it appearing here.

Drewes (1958) took EEG recordings of the occipital alpha rhythm under two conditions. Under the first condition (Task A) the subject sat with eyes open in a lighted room for a period of two minutes followed by a further two minutes with eyes closed. Under the second condition (Task B) the experimenter read out the following instructions:

Close your eyes. Form a mental picture of a large table and imagine yourself looking down on the top of the table. In the upper right hand corner of the table visualize a small triangle. Visualize a small circle on the lower right-hand corner of the table. Now visualize a small rectangle in the upper left-hand corner of the table. And in the lower left-hand corner of the table visualize a small square. Get a clear mental picture of the geometric figures in their respective corners. Keep your eyes closed. Now for the next two minutes I want you to visually manipulate those geometric figures from corner to corner. Try to visualize as many different combinations of these figures as you can without repeating any combination twice.

Subjects were allocated to one or other of three habitual imagery modes on the basis, not of alpha amplitude, but of alpha index. By alpha index is meant the percentage of time in seconds, or of distance in centimetres, that the alpha waves (8—13 c.p.s.) are present during the testing period. The criteria employed are shown in Table 4.3 facing.

TABLE 4.3

Drewes (1958) Alpha index criteria for classifying subjects into habitual imagery modes

Task	Visualizers		Responsives		Non visualizers	
	Eyes open	Eyes closed	Eyes open	Eyes closed	Eyes open	Eyes closed
A	$\leq 5\%$	$\leq 20\%$	$\leq 10\%$	$\geq 90\%$	$\geq 80\%$	$\geq 95\%$
B		$\leq 10\%$		$25\text{--}75\%$		$\geq 90\%$
Size of sample	27		54		21	

To keep the three experimental groups as pure as possible all subjects who failed to meet these criteria were rejected. The final sample consisted of 102 University students within the age range 18 to 19.

The mean WAIS full scale I.Q. for all subjects was approximately 120. Differences between the three subgroups were insignificant. In addition to the WAIS all subjects were given the Rorschach and the Guildford-Zimmerman test of spatial visualization.

The results may be summarized as follows:

The visualizers performed significantly better than the non-visualizers on the Digit Span, Digit Symbol, Block Design and Object Assembly subtests of the WAIS. Of the seventeen scores obtained from the Rorschach the visualizers produced significantly more W, FK and FC responses and were significantly superior on the Guildford-Zimmerman test of spatial visualization.

The non-visualizers were significantly better than the visualizers on the Similarities, Arithmetic, Picture Completion and Picture Arrangement subtests of the WAIS and produced significantly more FM, cF + c, and K responses on the Rorschach.

In all the research discussed so far two primary measures of alpha have been mentioned—alpha amplitude and the alpha index. Though several other measures have been used as well only one more will be mentioned here as it is somewhat different from the rest and may prove to be important in future research. Following a suggestion made by Shipton and

F

Walter (1957) it was reported by Slatter (1960) that the most common alpha frequency among habitual visualizers was 12 c.p.s. 'Of the 12 students with this dominant frequency, 11 were habitual visualizers, and all 12 records had average alpha amplitudes below 24.6μV.'

Some independent evidence which favours the utilization of this alpha frequency measure is provided by Gastaut (1954). He attempted to relate several characteristics of the alpha rhythm, including alpha frequency, to reports from other investigators concerning some associated personality character-istics. MacFarlane Smith (1964) comments on the similarity of the alpha classification proposed by Gastaut to that of Grey Walters and Table 4.4 below provides a summary of the suggested relationships.

TABLE 4.4

Tentative classification of alpha, personality and imagery characteristics

(Based upon a table presented by McFarlane Smith, 1964)

Alpha type Gastaut	Frequency of Alpha rhythm	Personality type	Image type Grey Walter
Hyperexcitability Syndrome: Rare and rapid alpha rhythms of low amplitude, grouped in short bursts of desynchronized activity	11–13 c.p.s.	Active independent, hypersensitive	Visualizer
Lability or versatility Syndrome: Rare alpha rhythm but associated with slower or more rapid waves or both	9–11 c.p.s.	Impatient, aggressive, intolerant	Mixed or responsive
Hypoexcitability Syndrome: Slow, strong, regular alpha rhythm of continuous high amplitude, no desynchronized intervals	8–11 c.p.s.	Passive, dependent, submissive, slow, calm, even tempered	Verbalizer

Though some direct evidence connecting high alpha frequency with low alpha amplitude has been cited by Mundy-Castle (1958) and by Slatter (1960) it would be interesting to investigate the relation between alpha frequency and a variety of 'arousal' measures. If the relation between alpha frequency and visual imagery is confirmed and if alpha frequency is less susceptible to changes in arousal level some of the confounding discussed earlier would disappear.

The last study to be mentioned in this section is one reported by Brown (1966). Self reports were obtained from 48 subjects concerning their visual imaging abilities. These reports, which were based on questionnaire data and interviews, were assessed by three independent judges. Of the subjects 9 were classified as habitual visualizers and another 8 as habitual non-visualizers. When these 17 subjects were instructed to imagine a previously-seen swinging pendulum as in the method employed by Deckert (1964), 7 of the 9 habitual visualizers exhibited pursuit eye movements compared with only 3 of the 8 habitual non-visualizers.

Though alpha amplitude declined in all the habitual visualizers and in only one of the habitual non-visualizers during the solution of mental arithmetic problems and the recall of familiar visual scenes the most interesting finding concerned the differential amount of alpha following in response to red photic flicker. 'In the habitual visualizers, EEG photic following was always attenuated during red presentations as compared to following to either blue or green, whereas in the habitual non-visualizers, EEG photic following was always enhanced with red flicker.'

No attempt has been made to survey all the relevant work on habitual imagery modes and their suggested correlates, nor on the relation of alpha blocking to visual imagery (e.g., Drever, 1955, 1958; Simpson, Paivio and Rogers, 1967). The main aim has been to show some of the problems that have arisen in utilizing characteristics of the alpha rhythm as measures of these modes. The following few paragraphs are intended to summarize the present position and to suggest what appear to be the more promising research leads for the future.

It is clear that Golla, Hutton and Grey Walter's (1943) 'working hypothesis' of a simple association between three distinct types of resting alpha rhythm and three habitual imaging modes has not been substantiated when the amplitude of the resting alpha rhythm has been used as the criterion. It has been amply demonstrated also, that conditions like anxiety, change in the stimulus and mental effort are likely to increase arousal level and produce a blocking of the alpha rhythm quite apart from the activity of visualizing.

For the practical purpose of classifying habitual imagery modes from such alpha characteristics as amplitude and duration, it would be necessary to monitor other indices of arousal level, such as respiration and body movements, to ensure that alpha changes are not attributable to non-imagery sources. The practical problem is to discover the criteria that will enable us to select habitual imagery groups which will in turn perform differentially on a variety of other tasks. The use of alpha frequency as a measure less susceptible to arousal changes should be explored further.

To improve the reliability of using alpha characteristics as a selection procedure, a more varied set of relatively simple tasks involving all degrees of visualizing and verbalizing should be standardized.

2. Classification based upon breathing patterns

As early as 1929, Golla and Antonovitch reported on the breathing records of sixty-seven subjects and concluded that visual imagery seemed to be associated with regular breathing, while verbal-auditory imagery was associated with more irregular breathing patterns. Further support for this observation was obtained by Wittkower (1934) and Paterson (1935). Whereas the earlier studies had used a pneumograph, Short (1953) used a thermo-couple placed below the nostrils to convert breath temperature into electrical impulses which in turn registered their variations on one channel of an EEG unit. Short used both a patient sample and seventy-five normal subjects. Before examining their breathing records he had classified them into predominantly visualizers and predominantly verbalizers on the basis of introspective reports while they were completing a number of mental tasks. Though the visualizers had regular breathing records whatever mental tasks they were engaged upon, the verbalizers also had regular breathing records when engaged upon spatial tasks. Clearly, a regular breathing record could result in theory not only from visual thinking but also from imageless thinking.

In part of a study reported by Chowdhury and Vernon (1964) a pneumograph was used to measure breathing patterns. After becoming accustomed to the apparatus each subject was given a series of six different mental tasks, each of which now followed by a brief introspective report. Scores on a regular-irregular dimension were calculated for each of the seventy subjects and correlated with their visual imagery scores on the Burt-Galton vividness of imagery questionnaire. A significant correlation of 0.378 was obtained.

In a study of the covert oral behaviour associated with the occurrence of auditory hallucinations McGuigan (1966) used 'specially constructed vacuum-type electrodes' to pick up muscle action potentials from the tongue. These electrodes do not impede normal speech and would appear to provide a valuable new technique for the study of the verbalizer.

3. *Classification based upon subject reports*

Evidence for a separation of imaging abilities into those which are predominantly verbal and those which are predominantly visual may be found in a variety of places ranging all the way from the anecdotal (Pear, 1937) through the systematic inter-viewing of selected subjects (Roe, 1951) to careful introspective studies like those of Griffitts (1927).

Verbal imagery as noted earlier may contain a variety of visual auditory and kinaesthetic images, and in the case of the last, sensations. It is relatively rare to see words as though they are written on a blackboard, or on a kind of endless band of tickertape. However, a classic example of this visual form is provided by Galton (1883).

One statesman has assured me that a certain hesitation in utterance, which he has at times, is due to his being plagued by the image of his manuscript speech with its original erasures and corrections. He cannot lay the ghost and he puzzles in trying to decipher it.

The more common forms of verbal imagery involve combina-tions of auditory and kinaesthetic imagery, and it is for these that the term 'inner speech' has been traditionally employed.

In the study by Griffitts (1927) the dominance of the visual, auditory and kinaesthetic elements in verbal imagery was measured. Eight different tasks were used and each subject was required to distribute seven points between each of the three modalities on the completion of each task. It was found that 76 % of the subjects had a predominance of inner speech, though some visual component was present in most of them. Among the conclusions were the following:

. . . when auditory and kinaesthetic are present in verbal imagery they are almost invariably present simultaneously. I found no clear case of the simultaneous presence of visual and kinaesthetic without any auditory. Visual and auditory may appear together with the kinaesthetic absent. These facts probably are to be explained as the results of language habits. Most of our first verbal experiences are auditory and kinaesthetic, and while talking these two elements are simultaneous and naturally become closely linked. At times we have experienced simultaneously the visual and auditory while watching the page as another reads aloud. But, while acquiring our language habits, if we experience the visual and kinaesthetic sensations simultaneously, auditory sensations are likely to be present also.

In a later part of his monograph Griffitts writes: 'it is probable that the majority of those who are said to belong to the "visual type" are "concrete" thinkers and that those classed as "auditory-motor" are "verbal" thinkers.' This notion of 'concrete' and 'verbal' thinking which is part of being an habitual visualizer or an habitual verbalizer is discussed by June Downey (1929). She writes,

It is an enlightening experience to gather records, as I have, of the variety of word experiences. Try out a list of one hundred words on a dozen different subjects and note the reaction you get . . . You will find no doubt the *dictionary minded* individual. The words you show him call up, in turn, definitions of their meaning, or, perhaps merely a synonym or antonym or a phrasal-completion of the word. You know him for his precision and fluency of language, his discrimination in choice of words. He is perhaps of a legal turn of mind . . . thinking in the abstract, reasoning in words as with counters, swiftly, skilfully, accurately. You will find the *concrete-minded* person for whom words are merely coin of the realm to be exchanged as rapidly as possible into concrete images. 'Fortitude' does not call up the synonymous term 'courage' but the picture of a mother singing quietly to her dying child.

74

More recently, Anne Roe (1951) studied the imagery of 61 eminent research scientists in the fields of biology, physics, psychology and anthropology. She asked them to describe the typical ways in which they carried on their thinking. From the detailed accounts obtained she found it possible to classify all of them into one or other of four groups. Twenty-two were essentially visualizers, while another 19 were essentially verbalizers. A further 13 were classified as imageless on the basis of such comments as: 'I just seem to vegetate—something is going on I don't know what it is'. The remaining 7 scientists were classified as mixed because they utilized both visual and verbal processes in their thinking. It is of interest that she found significantly more verbalizers among the psychologists and anthropologists and significantly more visualizers among the biologists and the physicists.

Memory imagery and other psychological processes

This final section on memory imagery has been reserved for a discussion of some empirical investigations which have a bearing upon a variety of other psychological problems. Memory images will be considered in relation to such processes as stimulus coding and retention, problem solving, interpersonal communication, and behaviour modifications associated with psychotherapy.

1. Stimulus coding and retention

Of the two principle ways of encoding a stimulus, verbal coding seems to be the most common. Harris and Haber (1963) in an unpublished pilot study found that 75 out of 77 subjects encoded a briefly presented visual stimulus in a verbal form and silently rehearsed it, in this form, until a report was called for. The remaining two subjects relied upon visual imagery.

Such proportions may be expected to vary considerably with the population chosen for investigation, though not so much, with the range of tasks chosen. In discussing visualizers and vocalizers in relation to their methods of encoding information to be remembered, Bartlett (1932) wrote: 'It is interesting to notice that where the same subjects took part in the different experiments their general methods remained the same, in spite of the differences of material employed and of other conditions.'

In the past (see Hunter, 1956) both verbal and image forms of encoding information have been used as the basis of mnemonic systems, and of the two the use of imagery appears to have been the more popular. Hill (1918) provides a useful classroom demonstration of the manner in which 25 or 30 (or 100) unrelated words or objects can be accurately registered, retained and recalled after only one presentation. The first step is to learn the set of 100 key words. This is made easy by providing a rational system of associations. Each word in the list has a natural association with a number: e.g., 1. AIR (A); 2. BAR (B); 3. CAR (C); 4. DAGGER (D). In addition a visual image should be formed for each key word.

To the writer, the word *Air* brings up a picture of the open heavens, atmosphere, blue sky. *Bar*, to him recalls a great sand bar he once saw on the seashore. *Car*, a passenger coach. *Dagger*, a silver paper cutter on the desk.

When once the set of key words has been learned other information can be encoded in terms of these 'imagery pegs'. The objects or words to be remembered should be exposed one at a time for long enough to form an image in relation to the numbered 'imagery peg.'

Each word heard must arouse in the experimenter's mind a definite image and this is to be related to the permanent images already formed for the mnemonic series, e.g., the reader first says *dog*. I think of my own dog, his colour, size, appearance, and in order to link the ideas with mnemonic 1. I try to think vividly of this dog sniffing the air on a light cloudless day . . . I thereupon dismiss the picture. I say 'now' or 'next' and the reader for his second word perhaps says *tree*. Mentally I portray a lone tree upon that sand bar . . . representing mnemonic 2. The next word is *brick*. I think of a railroad car . . . full of bricks, the car representing mnemonic 3. The more vivid the picture, even if it be ridiculous, the more promptly will each mental complex be recalled after the 25, 30, or more words have thus been heard and the ideas blended or associated.

At first thought it may appear surprising that with much use the 'imagery pegs' do not become cluttered with all the objects and words that have been hung upon them. In practice this does not seem to happen and the most plausible explanation is that each occasion on which the set of 'imagery pegs' is utilized is separately indexed. On occasion one, the mnemonic system might have been used as a classroom demonstration; on occasion two it could have been used to remember a shopping list; and so on. If the occasion is recalled then the corresponding series of fused images (imagery peg + object or word to be remembered) is recalled. When no occasion is recalled the series of 'imagery pegs' are clear of all past associated material and ready for use.

In a study by Smith and Noble (1965) a mnemonic system published by Furst (1957) was examined for its value in learning consonant-vowel-consonant lists. These lists were of low, medium and high association values (meaningfulness), with the high lists comprising actual words.

It was concluded that Furst's mnemonic technique has limited usefulness during the *acquisition* of a serial verbal list, and perhaps a significant facilitating effect on *retention*, provided the material to be recalled is of medium or low meaningfulness, but no efficacy for remembering highly meaningful materials learned under the present conditions.

The model for these mnemonic systems would seem to be a paired associate learning situation in which the standard list of imaged objects ('imagery pegs') comprises the stimulus words and the list of objects to be remembered comprises the response words. Each imaged object in the standard (stimulus) list is paired with an imaged object in the variable list (response). Allan Paivio and his colleagues at the University of Western Ontario have been concerned with the place of imagery in paired associate learning and have indirectly obtained some support for the principle underlying the mnemonic systems just discussed. Instead of the term 'imagery pegs' Paivio has referred to the stimulus items in paired associate learning as 'conceptual pegs'. He argued (Paivio, 1963) that the efficiency of words as 'conceptual pegs' depends upon their capacity to arouse images. A check on this expectation revealed that concrete nouns do arouse more imagery than abstract nouns. In addition the value of concrete nouns was found to be greater in facilitating recall when they were on the stimulus ('imagery' or 'conceptual peg') side of a paired associate list than on the response side. However, it was found

(Paivio, 1965) that the meaningfulness of concrete nouns is generally greater than that of abstract nouns, as measured by the frequency of association method. The greater efficiency of having concrete nouns as stimuli might therefore be attributed to their greater meaningfulness rather than to their greater power of arousing images. To test which of these two hypotheses is the more probable Yarney and Paivio (1965) equated lists of concrete and abstract nouns for meaningfulness and still found that concrete nouns aroused more imagery and were more effective stimulus words than were the abstract nouns. These findings suggest that imagery may be more effective than language, at least in situations where the material to be encoded is low on meaningfulness.

The language-versus-imagery encoding issue has also been studied by Ranken (1963, 1963a). He found that subjects who were instructed to encode a series of novel shapes in terms of relevant names made fewer errors in recalling the serial order in which the shapes had been presented. Subjects who had been instructed to visualize the shapes without using words made more errors in recalling the serial order, but made fewer errors in drawing the shapes from memory and in solving mental jigsaw puzzles involving the combination of several shapes. The greater accuracy of reproduction under the 'visualization' instruction compared with the 'naming' instruction parallels the results of Sheehan's studies reported earlier, in which it was found that more accurate reproductions of a stimulus pattern resulted from the instruction to 'image' it than from the instruction to 'recall' it.

Last to be mentioned, are some preliminary experiments by John Ross (1968) conducted at the University of Western Australia. These experiments have produced data that do not correspond to the usual findings of research on verbal learning. The subject was a female graduate student in psychology who exhibited no special ability to memorize before the study began. Using an imagery peg mnemonic procedure she recalled lists of up to 100 items, (nouns, adjectives and verbs) often with no errors at all. Retroactive and pro-active inhibition effects were virtually eliminated. In one experiment a list of 50 concrete nouns was read once at the rate of approximately one item every five seconds. The subject was then instructed to recall, verbally, the alternate items in serial order. No errors of content or order were made. The experimenter then assigned a new serial position to each of the 50 items and read them to the subject once again at the same rate as before. Two omissions were recorded when the alternate items from this re-ordered lists were recalled. Without warning, the subject was asked for written recall of the complete list of 50 items in its original order — only two errors were made, both omissions.

It is to be hoped that studies of the type reported in this section will bring about a better understanding of the conditions necessary for the most efficient functioning of the human memory.

2. *Problem solving*

As problem solving is dependent in part upon general intellectual ability, it will be useful to comment on the relationship between imagery and intelligence test scores. Several studies have investigated this problem, but no firm evidence is available. In a study in which school children were used as subjects, Carey (1915) obtained introspective reports on the vividness of their visual imagery and correlated these with measures of general intelligence. An insignificant negative correlation was obtained. In a study by Brower (1947) the Otis intelligence test (Higher Form B) and a self rating type measure of imaging ability were administered to thirty male and sixty-three female psychology students. Correlations between intelligence and self ratings on each modality of the imagery test were positive but insignificant.

Davis (1932) administered a battery of objective tests to groups of psychology students during normal class periods devoted to the discussion of imagery. Among these tests were: a tonal memory test, memory for simple geometrical figures, memory for words alike in sound but not in spelling, memory for words spelled alike but pronounced differently, a test of rhyming ability and a childhood free association test. In addition, scores on the Army Alpha intelligence test were available for these subjects. After completing the first test on tonal memory the subjects were asked,

Now state as accurately as possible how, in your opinion, you performed this test. (Slight pause.) Did you form a visual schema or pattern of the notes as you heard them the first time and again the second time, and compare the second pattern with the first? Some people report that they do this sort of test that way. (Slight pause.) Or were you aware of the movements, perhaps very slight movements, from your finger, or hand, or head, or eyes, or vocal cords, or from some other part of your body as the notes were played, and did you make your comparison of the two series of notes on the basis of those movements? Some people report that they do this sort of test in that way. (Slight pause.) Or did you concentrate on the sounds of the notes in the first series, and then carry them in your mind while you compared them with the notes of the second series? Some say they do it that way. Put down 'V' if a visual pattern was your method, 'K' if you were aware of movements and made your judgments on the basis of them, and 'A' if you made the comparison in terms of the sounds. If you used a combination of these or other processes, put down the letters which stand for the processes you used. If one of them seemed to you to be dominant over the others, underline it. If you are sure none of these entered into your performance of the test, put down 'none'. If you are uncertain, put down a question mark.

After each of the subsequent tests the experimenter simply said: 'Now tell as accurately as you can how you did it.'

Those who did best on the test of tonal memory had auditory imagery dominant, while those who did best on memory for geometrical figures were more likely to have visual imagery dominant. The tendency throughout was for subjects to have the relevant imagery mode dominant when they obtained high scores on the corresponding 'objective' test. As the Army Alpha intelligence test had low but positive correlations with most of these objective tests it might be tentatively inferred that the possession of relevant imagery and the capacity to utilize it as required, might also have a low but positive correlation with general intelligence.

From the three studies reported no consistent pattern of relationship emerges between imaging abilities and general intelligence. It might be tentatively concluded that in unselected populations no correlation will be found, but a specific test of this hypothesis should be undertaken before it is accepted. In addition it would be of particular interest to know whether the habitual visualizer and habitual verbalizer differ in their general intelligence. If the first tends to be more of a concrete thinker and the latter more of an abstract thinker does this reflect itself in relatively low and high scores on a 'g' saturated intelligence test?

Turning now to the specific part played by imagery in problem solving, it should be remembered at the outset that thinking can proceed without the presence of any detectable quasi-sensory content at all. Imageless thought most often accompanies the solution of routine tasks. As in perception and memory we utilize familiar knowledge for familiar purposes in familiar situations without being aware of it. Images of a concrete quasi-sensory type or of a verbal auditory-motor type are more likely to form when some barrier to further thought is encountered and the solution is not immediately available. An experimental demonstration of this fact was provided by Fox (1915).

The question has often been raised, and will continue to be raised for some time yet, as to whether the possession of vivid manipulable imagery in any particular modality has any special value to the thinker who possesses it. Humphrey (1951) concluded his own renew of thinking and its relation to imagery by noting that some imagery might on occasion be useful, but that extremely vivid imagery is likely to disrupt effective problem solving. Whether the emphasis should be on vividness as such, or whether its interaction with controllability is the significant factor, requires further research to elucidate. Of interest here is the suggestion by Grey Walter (1953) that the habitual visualizer might solve a concrete problem more quickly than an habitual verbalizer, but that a more abstract problem requiring elaborate mental pictures for its solution, slows down or confuses the visualizer. Too much dependence upon visual imagery may reduce the quality of performance on difficult tasks where highly generalized or abstract verbal thought processes might serve better. At the moment there is little reliable evidence to show what positive contribution to problem solving can come from the possession of vivid controllable memory imagery. However, a finding by Mawardi (cited by Hyman and Anderson, 1965) is of interest in this regard. She studied a group of professional problem solvers and found that their thinking showed constant alternation between abstract numerical and verbal modes of thought on the one hand and concrete imaging on the other. One of the advantages of this alternation appears to be in providing a basis for breaking an unproductive set towards the solution of a problem. Imagery provides another way of representing a problem to oneself and this in turn may provide the break-through to its solution. A related finding is reported by Rowan (1965) who writes:

Carnegie Tech. men tested a program that had been written for solving algebra word problems of the type that are given to high school students. This program 'translates' the word problems, step by step into algebraic equations. A number of algebra students do the same. But other youngsters first translate the English prose into a 'picture' of the physical situation and then translate this representation into equations. And those who perform this indirect rather than direct translation prove to be the more powerful problem-solvers.

The ability to obtain vivid voluntary images might also aid in problem solving through its association with independence of judgment. Schmeidler (1965) administered a revised form of Galton's classic 'breakfast table' questionnaire of imagery vividness to 170 male and 137 female students at the City College of New York. In addition all the students completed the eight item independence of judgment test which was found by Barron (1958) to discriminate between creative and non-creative adults in the same profession. The correlation between imagery and independence was $+0.21$ ($p < .01$) for the men and $+0.17$ ($p = .06$) for the women.

When all these provisional findings are considered in relation to other observations on imagery and problem solving, several questions arise. In discussing the imagery of research scientists (Roe, 1951) it appeared that thinkers in different disciplines had a preference for either verbalizing or visualizing their problem. There was little evidence from this study that high grade research scientists alternate the manner of representing problems to themselves; though some did. Would they be even more effective problem-solvers if they could utilize both forms of representation? Apart from the possible set-breaking value of having imagery and inner speech available when solving a particular problem, Short (1953) has suggested that a 'mixed' type like this also has an advantage when moving from the solution of a problem where verbalizing is perhaps more appropriate to the solution of a problem where the ability to visualize might be especially useful. However, in the study by Short and

Walter (1954) using stereognosis tasks, it was found that better performances were achieved by habitual verbalizers and habitual visualizers than by those who switched backwards and forwards between the two modes. As these stereognosis tasks required tactile recognition of shapes it might be argued that little of what is normally included under problem solving is involved. Nevertheless, it is clear that the value of an ability to switch modes, both within a problem and between different types of problem needs to be explored further.

Some evidence has been provided by educational psychologists in the Soviet Union that pupils who have relatively little capacity for school mathematics have a 'predominance of the visual imagery component of thinking over the verbal logical component'. Krutetski (1963) who reports this research, found that the verbal logical mode is a necessary though not a sufficient condition for better than average performance. Whether this finding would still hold if the visualizers and the verbalizers were matched on general intelligence if of special importance in interpreting these results.

3. *Interpersonal communication*

The possibility that different modes of thought might constitute a barrier to successful communication between people has often been suggested though little research has been undertaken so far. Lay (1897) mentions the difficulty of Protagoras and Socrates in understanding one another and suggests that this may have been due to the predominance of kinaesthesis in the verbal imagery of Protagoras compared with the predominance of auditory verbal imagery in Socrates' thought. It will be remembered that Socrates always *heard* the voice of his Daemon. Lay then put forward some general advice that: 'if one is auditory-linguistic he should never enter into an argument with the motor-linguistic person, as on all topics except the most concrete facts, either will inevitably fail, completely, to understand the other.'

Grey Walter (1953) suggests that much intolerance and misunderstanding may arise when habitual visualizers and habitual verbalizers are discussing a problem.

Drewes (1958) writes,

It would appear that extreme 'imagery' differences could plausibly lead to incompatible modes of communication and perhaps dis-harmony and dispute. Imagine a teacher who is an extreme non-visualizer trying to communicate his concepts and ideas in terms of abstractly oriented symbols to an extreme visualizer, who tries to 'make contact' through vivid visual patterns of thought. The student might think the 'transmitter' abstruse, and the teacher might think the 'receiver' obtuse.

McKellar (1965) quotes one of his correspondents who seems to have felt intensely about this difficulty which arises from our hidden differences: 'It is so funny, that "but surely everybody thinks like me" feeling. It does cause quite a shock sometimes to find out that nobody in one's immediate invironment does.'

An attempt to investigate one aspect of this communication problem was made by Richardson (1965). One basis for com-munication difficulties would exist if it could be shown that habitual visualizers are more idiosyncratic in the connotative meanings that they attach to words and phrases than are habitual verbalizers. The argument in support of the hypo-thesis is based upon the fact that words and their meanings are created and validated in a social context, while images and their meanings are personal creations and are never validated in this way. Habitual verbalizers use words for interpersonal communication and also, on occasion, use words in the form of inner speech for their own self-conscious intrapersonal com-munications. Under these conditions minimal distortion of meaning is likely to occur. For the habitual visualizer on the other hand, words are just as necessary for interpersonal communication, but for purposes of intrapersonal communica-tion, translation from a verbal to a visual mode of represen-tation and back again is also necessary. Under these conditions there is a greater opportunity for idiosyncratic meanings to be created.

Some indirect evidence already existed for this hypothesis though it was not known to the writer at that time. Kuhlman (1960) studied the place of imaging in children's thought, using tests of visualizing efficiency as measures of imagery. High and low 'imagery' children were asked to reproduce ambiguous drawings each of which had been labelled with the name of a familiar object. When the influence of drawing ability and memory for visual designs had been controlled, it was found that the reproductions produced by the high imagery children showed less convergence towards the named objects than did the reproduction of the low imagery children. In effect, the visualizers were more idiosyncratic in their responses and the non-visualizers were more stereotyped in theirs.

A direct test of the hypothesis required the selection of a group of habitual visualizers and habitual verbalizers. A typical selection procedure was based upon scores on the Sheehan test of imagery vividness and on subjective reports of thought processes during the solution of four tasks used in previous imagery research by Stewart and MacFarlane Smith (1958). At different times four groups of visualizers and verbalizers were selected, though the methods of selection varied slightly in each.

To measure differences in the connotative meanings of words and phrases a set of twelve concepts was constructed and rated by the visualizers and verbalizers using the standard instructions for the Semantic Differential proposed by Osgood, Suci and Tannenbaum (1957).

The hypothesis was tested by obtaining the mean ratings on each concept separately for each of the two groups; then the standard deviations were calculated on each concept separately for each of the two groups. As the ratings provide data for three dimensions of meaning on each concept (Evaluation, Potency and Activity), the distribution of standard deviations for each concept on each of three dimensions could be compared for the visualizers and verbalizers. If the hypothesis is true that 'habitual visualizers are more idiosyncratic in the connotative meanings that they attach to words and phrases than are habitual verbalizers', then the size of the standard deviation for each concept rated by the group of visualizers should be greater than the size of the standard deviation for the same concepts rated by the group of verbalizers. Data from the most confirmatory of the four pilot studies are shown in Table 4.5 below.

It should be emphasized that the investigation described here is chiefly intended to illustrate just one approach to the study of imagery and interpersonal communication. The major difficulties that have been found so far concern the selection of habitual visualizers and verbalizers and the elimination of other correlated factors that might provide an equally

TABLE 4.5

Comparison of habitual visualizers and habitual verbalizers on degree of idiosyncrasy (measured by standard deviations) on three dimensions of connotative meaning for each of 12 concepts (words and phrases)

Concept	Evaluation			Potency			Activity		
	Verb.	Vis.	Diff.	Verb.	Vis.	Diff.	Verb.	Vis.	Diff.
Dollar	1·04	1·35	+·31	0·44	0·68	+·24	0·81	0·68	−·13
Sky	0·75	0·56	−·19	0·73	0·66	−·07	0·69	1·22	+·53
Knife	0·60	0·62	+·02	0·52	0·56	+·04	0·79	0·97	+·18
Japanese	0·81	1·36	+·55	0·57	0·56	−·01	1·03	0·82	−·21
Australian	0·44	0·73	+·29	0·66	0·58	−·08	0·41	1·06	+·65
Filipino	0·52	0·62	+·10	0·41	0·75	+·34	0·47	0·92	+·45
'Give me liberty . . .'	1·08	1·56	+·48	0·53	0·56	+·03	0·85	1·01	+·16
'The yellow bees . . .'	0·73	0·74	+·01	0·60	0·74	+·14	0·81	1·30	+·49
'Light heard as . . .'	0·65	0·64	−·01	0·53	0·50	−·03	0·72	0·80	+·08
Justice	0·57	1·49	+·92	0·76	0·71	−·05	0·67	0·82	+·15
God	0·94	0·55	−·39	0·37	0·78	+·41	0·60	0·99	+·39
Science	0·58	0·81	+·23	0·68	0·86	+·18	0·60	0·68	+·08
	T = 15·5 p<·05 (one tailed)			T = 21·5 n.s.			T = 10 p<·01 (one tailed)		

Subjects: First year Psychology students
Visualizers: (N = 10)
Verbalizers: (N = 11)

satisfactory explanation of the results. Though intelligence as measured by the ACER B40 test does not appear to correlate with the visualizer-verbalizer dimension, it is possible that scores on a vocabulary test might. If it were found that verbalizers had better vocabulary scores than visualizers then the lower variability of concept meanings for the verbalizers might signify no more than a clearer understanding of the denotative meanings of these concepts.

One other type of study should be mentioned in which richness of fantasy has been found to correlate with general persuasibility (Hovland and Janis, 1959). Richness of fantasy was measured by an 11-item questionnaire which included several questions related to imagery, e.g., 'At times when you are hoping that some pleasant experience will occur, do you ever imagine it so vividly in your own mind that you can practically see and feel what the experience would be like?' General persuasibility was defined as: 'a person's readiness to accept social influence from others irrespective of what he knows about the communicator or what it is that the communicator is advocating.' In a sample of 86 adolescent boys a significant correlation of 0.21 was obtained between persuasibility and richness of fantasy. In a sample of 96 adolescent girls the correlation was insignificant (0.01).

The measure of richness of fantasy is not, of course, a pure measure of voluntary imaging ability nor of spontaneous imagery, and this study is included merely to indicate another way in which imagery may be significant in communication and in attitude change.

A further linkage between richness of fantasy and persuasibility is suggested by one of the results obtained in a study concerned with imagination and waiting ability in young children (Singer, 1961). On the basis of structured interviews with a group of 40 children aged between 6 and 9 years he reports a tendency for more of the high—than of the low—fantasy children to be either first born or only children. As the most consistent finding in almost all the literature on birth order effects has shown a significant association between being a first born or only child and being more influencible (e.g., Warren, 1966) the place of imagery and richness of fantasy in this pattern deserves further exploration and interpretation. Another line of investigation would be to study the differential effectiveness of role playing on attitude change when the independent variable was a measure of imagery vividness and control. Does successful role playing require some minimum capacity to image the role beforehand and to 'see' and 'feel' oneself enacting it? Most of the writers in the social interaction tradition imply that this kind of an ability is involved. A wide range of relevant quotations from writers such as C. H. Cooley and G. H. Mead are provided in an article by Stark (1966).

4. *Behaviour modifications associated with psychotherapy*

The place of imagery in bringing about psychotherapeutic changes has not been investigated in any systematic way, though it is frequently discussed by writers on psychotherapy (e.g., Armstrong, 1953; Reyher, 1963). The purpose of this section is to present some of the relevant observations that have been made by therapists of different theoretical orientations and to suggest the desirability of incorporating measures of imaging ability in studies of the efficacy of these therapeutic procedures. The three psychotherapeutic approaches to be discussed are those of—psycho-synthesis, hypno-therapy and behaviour therapy.

(a) Psycho-synthesis: The procedures underlining the use of this technique are outlined by Gerard (1964) but include controlled visualization as an essential part of the total process.

In controlled symbolic visualization, although some of the details may be spontaneous, the basic pictorial content is specified in advance. A preparatory state consists of sitting in a comfortable chair, closing the eyes and achieving as relaxed a state as possible . . . Attention is withdrawn as much as possible from bodily processes and extraneous thoughts and focussed upon the specified symbol, or symbolic scene, which is being created in the 'mind's eye'.

These conditions are of the kind that are most likely to arouse imagination images and in fact one of the standard procedures is called 'the guided daydream'. However, the subject is required to sit on a chair rather than to rest on a couch for the express purpose of maintaining 'ego control over imaginative processes.'

Many types of symbol are used, depending upon the problem, the client and the stage of therapy. A symbol of growth may be introduced for example, One client was asked to visualize a seed.

The tree started to grow and wanted to grow so fast that the trunk was not strong enough to support the branches. It never became a tree. Instead it became a vine which stayed close to the ground, like a clinging vine, which represented vividly the way the patient depended on others. To have him start allowing for a natural growth was part of the process of therapy with this individual.

As with dreams and verbal free associations, this would seem to be another way in which significant personal problems can be represented, externalized and interpreted. In other situations, the therapist asks the client to imagine a scene, e.g., lying on top of a blanket on the beach. The client is asked to describe what it feels like; then he might be requested to sit up in imagination and describe the beach; then to move into the sea and swim out far from the shore. These explorations of thought and feeling require control over visual imaging and presumably the habitual verbalizer would not have much chance of benefiting greatly from these procedures.

(b) Hypno-therapy: As hypnosis is a prerequisite of several forms of hypnotherapy (e.g., Brenman and Gill, 1947; Kline, 1952; Halpern, 1962, 1964) the findings of Sutcliffe (1965) and his colleagues at Sydney University are of special interest. Using the short form of the Betts test of imagery vividness and both the Stanford Hypnotic Susceptibility Scale (Form C) and another hypnotic susceptibility scale of their own devising, it was found that: 'Vividness of imagery is necessary but not sufficient for the characterization of the hypnotizable personality'. Hypnotizable subjects have vivid imagery but not all subjects with vivid imagery are hypnotizable.

In relation to this finding, some unpublished data obtained while the writer was a visitor at the University of Kansas is of interest. One of the best predictors of hypnotizability is the body sway test of primary suggestibility; in fact, it has been argued that when following the experimenter's instructions to 'fall forward' the person who begins to sway is already in a light hypnotic trance.

As in the Sutcliffe study, subjects who sway most might be expected to possess vivid imagery, though not all of those with vivid imagery will manifest much sway. What other variables interact with vividness of imagery to facilitate sway for some and to inhibit it in others? One variable that seemed an obvious candidate for investigation was imagery control. It was argued that the subject who has vivid controlled imagery may easily dismiss the 'falling' imagery suggested by the experimenter and for this reason show relatively little sway. On the other hand a subject who has vivid uncontrollable imagery might be expected to find difficulty in disposing of the 'falling' imagery and might therefore show more sway than the others. The vivid imagers who sway most (are hypnotizable?) are the ones who cannot control their imagery, while the vivid imagers who show little sway (are not hypnotizable?) are those who can control their imagery.

Following this line of reasoning it was predicted that the mean amount of sway for the four high/low combinations of vividness and controllability should show the following order: Vivid uncontrolled>Weak uncontrolled>Vivid controlled> Weak controlled. Having weak controlled imagery should lead to least sway because the suggestion to image oneself falling would have very little effect and what effect it had, could be easily controlled.

With the co-operation of staff and students a total of forty-two student subjects completed the short form of the Betts test of imagery vividness and the Gordon test of imagery control, plus a 90 second test of body sway, using a tape recorded set of 'falling' instructions. Scores on vividness and controllability were split at the median to form the four combinations. All falls and body movements of 10 inches or more were arbitrarily scored as 10 inches and the mean amount of sway calculated for each of the four groups.

As can be seen from Table 4.6 the mean number of inches moved by each of the four imaging groups is in the order predicted though the difference between the terminal groups fails to achieve a satisfactory level of significance ($t=1.24$) and the standard deviations of all the groups are not equivalent.

As noted in relation to several other studies reported in this chapter the interaction effects of vividness and controllability deserves more investigation. This is as true in this difficult field of predicting hypnotizability as it is in the other areas discussed.

(c) Behaviour therapy: In the desensitization or reciprocal

TABLE 4.6

Means and standard deviations of sway in inches for each of four combinations of imagery vividness and imagery control

| Sway | IMAGERY | | | |
	Vivid Uncontrolled Imagery	Weak Uncontrolled Imagery	Vivid Controlled Imagery	Weak Controlled Imagery
Mn.	4·30	4·00	3·33	3·00
S.D.	2·56	3·18	2·22	1·89
n	10	12	12	8

inhibition procedures developed by Wolpe (1958), the deeply relaxed patient is required to visualize a carefully graded series of subjectively unpleasant situations. The situations which initially provoke little anxiety are to be visualized first and, as tolerance increases, those which are higher in the anxiety hierarchy are visualized. Ultimately the most distressing scene in this hierarchy can be imagined and tolerated without anxiety. When faced with the real life counterparts of the imagined scenes many patients are no longer fearful. Apart from phobic reactions success has been claimed for this method in the treatment of exhibitionism (Bond and Hutchinson, 1960), chronic frigidity (Lazarus, 1963) and many other behaviour disorders.

In a discussion of the crucial procedural factors in desensitization therapy Lazarus (1964) wrote: 'An essential prerequisite for successful desensitization is the patient's ability to picture the imagined scenes sufficiently clearly, vividly and realistically for them to evoke anxiety at the outset.' How clear, vivid and realistic must these 'imagined scenes' be if desensitization is to occur? Would it be impossible for the habitual verbalizer to benefit from this form of treatment? It would seem, once again, that the capacity to form and control vivid images is an important individual difference variable.

Conclusion

To the question: 'What part does memory imagery play in the experience and behaviour of man?' the answer must still be: 'We don't know'; but that it plays some part in many of the psychological processes of central interest to a science of psychology seems much more probable today than it did thirty years ago.

The major problem facing imagery research has always been, and still is, the problem of measurement, but some promising tools are being developed. Of these the following require particular mention and further investigation:

1. The short form of the Betts test of *imagery vividness* administered to individuals or small groups after careful checking that the nature of an image is understood. It is of particular importance that studies be conducted to find out the influence of response sets such as acquiescence on self report measures, like this one and that of Gordon (1949).
2. The Gordon test of *imagery control* could perhaps be improved by the addition of suitable items to cover other sense modalities than vision. If scores derived from Necker cube reversal rates are found in future research to have very high correlations with the Gordon test, then it might serve as an alternative measure of *imagery control*.
3. The use of alpha frequency in conjunction with alpha amplitude for the selection of *habitual visualizers* and the use of breathing records for the selection of *habitual verbalizers* needs further experimental work.

McGuigan's (1966) technique for recording muscle action currents in the tongue is also likely to provide a valuable method for detecting the presence of verbalizing tendencies. The development of a standard testing procedure which will ultimately enable research workers everywhere to produce cumulative meaningful studies is needed urgently.

Chapter 5

IMAGINATION IMAGERY

A FEW words of explanation are necessary for bringing together under one heading several forms of imagery that are usually treated separately. Among these separate forms are the following: hypnagogic imagery (e.g., McKellar and Simpson, 1954); perceptual isolation imagery (e.g., Vernon, 1963); hallucinogenic drug imagery (e.g., Thale, Westcott and Salomon, 1950); photic stimulation imagery (e.g., Freedman and Marks, 1965); pulse current imagery (e.g., Knoll and Kugler, 1964); sleep deprivation imagery (e.g., Bliss and Clark, 1962); meditation imagery (e.g., Pinard, 1957).

The main difference between these forms of imagery is in the antecedent conditions that arouse them and not in the phenomenal attributes that appear in the subject's report. Whereas relatively clear distinctions mark off after-imagery, eidetic imagery and memory imagery from one another, the literature on the forms of imagery listed above has fallen into a terminological chaos. Some attempt to bring them together under a single name seems worthwhile.

It remains now to justify the use of imagination imagery as the integrating term. Imagination imagery has been used traditionally to contrast with memory imagery, though without any generally agreed-upon criteria to differentiate it (see: Perky, 1910; Ogden, 1913). Memory-images are usually defined as images which refer to particular events or occasions having a personal reference. The *memory-image* of a hammer that I now have in my mind's eye is of a particular claw hammer that is resting on the top shelf of an old bookcase at the back of my garage. The visual image of a hammer of no particular weight or type and with no other personal reference marks would be a *generic image*. But the mental picture of a hammer with a solid gold head and a smooth ivory handle would be an *imagination-image* because I had never seen such a hammer until a moment ago when I constructed an image of it.

This traditional distinction between memory and imagination imagery is illustrated in one of the experiments on spontaneous imagery conducted by Perky (1910). Spoken words and sentences were used as stimuli and the subjects were instructed to report on the imagery that was evoked.

It soon appeared that a good proportion of the images thus aroused were of two sharply different kinds. There were, on the one hand, images of recognized and particular things, figuring in a particular spatial context, on a particular occasion, and with definite personal reference; and there were, on the other hand, images with no determination of context, occasion, or personal reference—images of things recognized, to be sure, but not recognized as this or that particular and individual object. The former were evidently 'images of memory'; the latter both by positive and negative character were 'images of imagination'.

This then, is the traditional distinction; but it is some of Perky's additional observations that provide the main justification for applying the term imagination imagery to all the varieties of imagery discussed here. Imagination images tend to be *novel, substantial, vividly coloured*, when in the visual mode, and involve 'concentrated and quasi-hypnotic attention with inhibition of associations'. Some of the typical observations made by the subjects in Perky's study are as follows; the images were said to be—'more brilliant than emeralds', 'more real than reality', 'greener than any grass', 'one part stands out very clear; beyond it shades off into a fog or haze'. These subjects were presumably normal and awake yet the quality of imagery has the *novelty*, the *vividness of colour* and *clarity of detail* that have been remarked upon by so many of the subjects in the other studies to be discussed. Imagery which is voluntarily constructed to achieve novelty and which lacks vividness of colour and clarity of detail has been included under the general heading of memory imagery. Thus in the present discussion some of the traditional distinctions are being ignored in favour of the italicized qualities just mentioned.

Having indicated the reason for using the blanket term

'imagination imagery' it remains to review some of the major antecedent conditions known to produce it. Some consideration will be given to the additional conditions that distinguish an hallucination from what in other respects might be called an imagination image. Finally an attempt will be made to outline the conditions that appear to be common to all methods of producing imagination imagery.

Conditions known to be associated with the occurrence of imagination images

HYPNAGOGIC IMAGERY

Hypnagogic images may occur in any sense modality, but their defining characteristic is their time of onset during the twilight state between wakefulness and sleep. The naming of this phenomenon is attributed to Alfred Maury (1861) the French dream investigator who used the term 'illusion hypnagogique'. The term hypnopompic was first used by Myers (1903) to describe the imagery that sometimes occurs in the drowsy state between sleeping and waking. This hypnopompic imagery was said to be a persistence of normal dream imagery into this half waking state. As no important criteria separate the hypnagogic from the hypnopompic image the term hypnagogic will be used throughout.

The range of these subjective visual phenomena is very great and some examples have been taken from Leaning (1926) who has provided one of the best discussions of hypnagogic imagery.

1. *Meaningless images*

(a) Formless patches and flashes of light: 'Streams and patches of what seems to be a light flocculent matter'; 'Clouds of brilliant light seemed to roll and fade away before my closed eyes'; Flights of 'bright golden sparks'.

(b) Geometric forms: 'Patterns of perfect symmetry and geometrical regularity, both latticed, rhomboidal and circular'.

2. *Meaningful images*

(a) Single objects without background: Faces, either ugly or

95

beautiful are especially common; 'As a child and up to twenty years, I frequently saw large hideous faces a foot long, mouthing'; 'A face more lovely than any painting I have ever seen'; 'Hideous and terrifying'.

(b) Integrated scenes: 'In the case of landscapes the clouds roll aside and have the effect of revealing something already there'. This is very similar to the way in which crystal visions are experienced; 'There are two figures, a girl and a young man with a bicycle, she leaning on it, he kneeling at her feet. At the moment he is putting on his cap.'

Because some of the meaningless images closely resemble such objects as wheels, flowers, or snakes, these meaningful names may be applied to them. When subjects are asked to draw what they have seen and to give a careful literal description, it becomes clear that many of them have actually seen no more than a meaningless geometrical form. It is important that subjects are aware of this distinction when making their reports. However, it sometimes happens that what is seen initially as a meaningless geometrical form suddenly becomes a meaningful image. When this closure phenomenon occurs it is frequently difficult to return to seeing it as no more than a meaningless shape.

Before summarizing the main attributes of hypnagogic imagery, a more complete description will be quoted from the personal experience of the psychologist, Howard C. Warren (1921). He writes:

In a dark room with eyes closed a definite scene will appear before me in apparently as bright an illumination as daylight. I seem to be looking through my closed eyelids. The scene is apparently as real, as vivid, as detailed as an actual landscape. The phenomenon lasts not more than a minute. I have never been able to hold it long enough to notice any change or movement. It is a scene—not a happening. The two most vivid cases occurred quite automatically, either as I was dozing off and for some reason came back to consciousness, or immediately on waking during the night.

Once the scene was a tropical landscape, with palm trees and a body of water. It was clear and detailed and appeared so real that I was surprised to find it unchanged by winking.

From the age of at least eight years up until he was about 12 he experienced vivid imagery of constantly changing coloured patterns. He deliberately cultivated this imagery and up to the age of 18 he frequently imaged human figures and objects from these coloured patterns. At about this age his environment changed and he gave up the practise of imaging.

For many years my visualizing capacity was little used and seems to have degenerated, although I worked considerably with visual after-sensations. Within the past two years I have endeavoured to renew the practice of visualizing with closed eyes. At first the results were meagre; I saw only retinal light and fleeting after sensations. Gradually, the visualizing power has returned, and I am able to picture scenes voluntarily though not so vividly as in adolescence. I obtain these visualizations by concentrating the attention on the retinal field, endeavouring to form pictures out of what I see, and projecting them into a real scene. At first I see only the play of indefinite retinal light, which I weave into a picture with the help of imagination. Then all at once the picture becomes vividly real for an instant. I have never succeeded in prolonging these images. The effort to observe them attentively always throws them back into their former state; and often the attempt to control them voluntarily has the same result.

Griffitts (1927) reports that when visualizing objects like a rose or a flag his subjects would sometimes have imagination images which developed on the basis of 'retinal lights'.

The great majority of reported images are meaningful and typically show several of the five characteristics discussed below. The quality of *autonomy* is perhaps the most salient one; the images appear and follow their own course independent of the experiencer's will. As McKellar (1957) has observed 'they may surprise their authors by their highly creative and unreproductive character'. Though visual hypnagogic images may be uncoloured it is most common for them to be described as *vividly coloured* and they typically appear with *super distinctness of detail*. These images are of *brief duration*, ranging from a fraction of a second to a couple of minutes and often succeed one another in rapid succession. *Changes in shape or size* are not uncommon and the imaged face or other object may drift across the visual field or appear to approach closer and closer from some position directly in front of the observer. As might be expected these lateral movements are often associated with movements of the eye.

Attempts to survey particular populations have arrived at

different estimates. Though many factors might be expected to influence the outcome of such surveys, not the least of them is getting people to admit to having subjective experiences which they often believe to be abnormal.

Partridge (1898) asked 826 children to describe what they saw at night after their eyes were closed but before falling asleep. Though little trust can be put in the detailed results obtained, it is clear that the full range of meaningless and meaningful phenomena were reported by these children. Approximately 59 % of those in the 13 to 16 year age group reported hypnagogic images compared with approximately 64 % among the 6 year olds. On the basis of her review of earlier studies and of her own findings Leaning (1926) estimated that about one-third of the general population have at some time had a visual hypnagogic image. In a more recent study of 182 Aberdeen university students McKellar and Simpson (1954) report that 64 (35 %) of them had vivid autonomous visual images in the half awake state that precedes sleep; 4 said they had them regularly, 8 often, and 52 occasionally. Hypnagogic images in the auditory mode, most often voices or music, were slightly more frequent. Altogether, 78 subjects (43 %) reported auditory hypnagogic imagery; 4 regularly, 18 often and 56 occasionally. None of the above figures quoted from McKellar and Simpson's study include reports of hypnopompic imagery. The evidence suggests that all modalities of hypnagogic imagery may occur more frequently among children than among adolescents or adults and according to Kanner (1957) they 'play a prominent role, and are of a frightening nature in night terrors'. There is some evidence from a perceptual isolation study by Zuckerman et al (1962) that subjects who obtain images in one modality may be more likely to experience similar hypnagogic type images in other modes. For example, these authors report a correlation of 0.49 between imagery scores in the visual and auditory modes. It not infrequently happens that an auditory image may accompany a visual image. One of Freedman's (1962) sensory deprivation subjects observed:

One of the more peculiar images that I saw with music was . . . looking up at a wooden shelf, not very big, and watching the shelf, and listening to the music, and then the shelf started to wave in rhythm to the music in a very plastic fashion.

Similar cases of combined visual and auditory imagery are reported by Tyrrell (1953) in his book on apparitions. In the following example a tactile element was also involved:

... the percipient heard her name called three times and answered, thinking it was her uncle. The third time she recognized the voice of her mother who had been dead sixteen years. I said, 'Mama!' She then came round the screen near my bedside with two children in her arms, and placed them in my arms and put the bedclothes over them, and said, 'Lucy, promise to take care of them, for their mother is just dead' . . . I remained, feeling the children to be still in my arms, and fell asleep. When I awoke there was nothing.

It is of course possible that this entire episode is just a vivid nocturnal dream.

It is worth noting that Purdy's (1936) eidetic subject also reported having imagery combined from several modalities. 'When she forms a picture of ocean waves breaking on the shore, she has eidetic imagery of the sound and smell of the sea.'

From what has been reported on hypnagogic imagery so far it is clear that little in the way of measurement has been attempted. Few investigators have gone beyond the stage of naturalistic observation and simple enumeration of frequencies. The main phenomenal attributes of the experience are known, what is now wanted are the kind of experimental procedures that have been applied so successfully to the study of dreams.

An important beginning has been made in a study by Foulkes, Spear and Symonds (1966) who used an EEG measure to define the hypnagogic state. The subjects in the relevant part of this experiment were awakened during the descending Stage I EEG and questioned on what had been passing through their minds immediately prior to awakening. When the tape-recorded answers to this and other subsidiary questions were rated on an eight point (0—7) scale of dreamlike fantasy, significant differences in personality were found between those whose reports resulted in high ratings and those who were rated low. A high rating meant that a subject had described some scene or event that he saw and believed to be taking place outside himself. A low rating meant that a subject had reported nothing (0) or had in his mind some conceptual everydayish content (2).

Personality measures were obtained from the California

Personality Inventory and from the TAT. Those subjects who had the most dreamlike hypnagogic imagery were found to be psychologically healthier; they had greater social poise and were less rigidly conformist and more self accepting; they also showed greater creative achievement.

Those subjects who were rated low and had no hypnagogic imagery had a typical authoritarian syndrome and emerged as rigid, conventional, intolerant and anti-intraceptive.

When awkenings were arranged during Stage I REM periods of normal sleep it was found that ratings on the dream-like fantasy scale were uncorrelated with the ratings obtained during the hypnagogic stage. Subjects with high ratings (dreamlike fantasy) reported during the nocturnal awakenings obtained test results indicating especial concern with the problem of impulse control.

In a provisional interpretation of their findings the authors write:

It appears, then, that the hypnagogic dream might profitably be viewed as an ego-controlled excursion into inner thoughts and feelings following the ego's voluntary decathexis of sensory input from the external world. Subjects with rigid defences against impulse life tend to resist any encroachment of such regressive mental content upon wakeful levels of ego functioning, and thus experience little dreamlike content at sleep onset. The nocturnal dream, on the other hand, may be viewed as the ego's involuntary response to unconscious impulses and anxieties which become active during REM sleep. Subjects with egos lacking adequate defences against impulse life tend to be overwhelmed by it during REM sleep, hence experience especially vivid REM-sleep dreams.

PERCEPTUAL ISOLATION IMAGERY

Brownfield (1965) lists a total of twenty-five terms that have been used by different writers to describe the situation in which the quality and quantity of sensory input to a subject has been reduced. No accepted distinctions exist between these terms though Brownfield attempts to make one between *perceptual isolation* and *sensory deprivation*. While perceptual isolation is defined as a situation in which stimulation is boring, mono-tonous or invariant, but present to some degree, sensory isolation is defined as a situation in which stimulation is absent or markedly reduced. By these definitions the majority of studies have been concerned with perceptual isolation rather than sensory deprivation and for present purposes this is the generic term that will be applied.

A similar proliferation of terms has occurred as each investigator has sought to describe the experiences reported by his subjects. In the very first investigation by Bexton, Heron and Scott (1954) they were called 'visual' or 'auditory images'. Since then they have been called 'hallucinations' by Vernon (1958), a type of 'hypnagogic imagery' by Freedman, Grunebaum, Stare and Greenblatt (1962), 'reported visual sensations' by Myers and Murphy (1962) and 'non-object-bound' (n.o.b.) sensory phenomena by Scheibel and Scheibel (1962).

Some workers like Jack Vernon of Princeton University use very precise criteria for which the term 'visual hallucination' is technically correct. His criteria were as follows:

(1) the experience must have an 'out-thereness', just like any visual experience of the real world, (2) the one experiencing the hallucination must be able to scan, to attend selectively to, the various parts of the experience, (3) it must not be producible at the will of the subject, (4) the subject must not be able to terminate it, and (5) it must, for all purposes, 'fool' the observer with its realism (1963).

Other workers like Scheibel and Scheibel (1962) use a more general term like 'non-object-bound sensory phenomena' without worrying whether the subject believes in the reality of his imagery or whether he doesn't. It is perhaps worth emphasizing at this point that though hallucinations are most frequently associated with such pathological conditions as the functional and organic psychoses, they do occur in otherwise normal subjects. For example, during an eight hour perceptual isolation study reported by Freedman *et al* (1962), 'one presumably normal subject tried to eat an "imaged" salad'. However, it is more frequent for the subject who obtains imagination images under conditions of perceptual isolation to be aware that what he sees or hears does not have reality status. The problem of differentiating the hallucination from all other forms of imagination imagery will be considered at the end of this chapter.

As with the other circumstances under which imagination imagery occurs, a wide range of meaningless and meaningful experiences are reported. For example, Zuckerman (1964) after reviewing the literature on perceptual isolation concluded:

The median percentage of Ss reporting unstructured visual sensations in fifty-one experimental groups was 43%, and the median percentage for more structured or meaningful visual sensations was 19%. Comparable percentage for reported auditory sensations were 53% and 15%.

Though Freedman *et al* failed to find any sequence from less to more complexity, Myers and Murphy (1962) found that complexity of imagery was ordered on a four-step Guttman scale. Subjects always reported less complex images before reporting the more complex. There seems to be no logical reasons why such an ordering should be expected but it happens that this same order was found in the original studies conducted at McGill University. In reading Hebb's (1954) account given below, the ordering is perhaps of less importance than the description of the meaningless and meaningful images that were reported. Hebb writes:

It appears that the activity has a rather regular course of development from simple to complex. The first symptom is that the visual field, when the eyes are closed, changes from a dark to a light colour; next there are reports of dots of light, lines or simple geometrical patterns. All 14 subjects reported such imagery (in runs lasting from two to six days) which was a new experience to them. The next step reported by 11 subjects is seeing something like wallpaper patterns. Then came isolated objects without backgrounds, reported by 7 out of 14, and finally integrated scenes usually containing dreamlike distortions, reported by 3 of the 11. In general the subjects were surprised by these phenomena, and then were amused or interested, waiting for what they would see next. Later, some subjects found them irritating, and complained that their vividness interfered with sleep.

There seems to be little doubt that this description has reference to the same phenomena as those that have been called hypnagogic imagery, photic stimulation imagery, mescalin imagery, sleep deprivation imagery, pulse current imagery, and concentration imagery.

More research effort has been expended in the attempt to discover the necessary and sufficient conditions for the occurrence of perceptual isolation imagery than on any other form of imagination imagery. To give some idea of the situational and subject variables that have been investigated and of the main findings obtained so far, it will be useful to spend a little time in reviewing this work.

It was natural that most of the early research effort should be expended on a search for the conditions within the perceptual isolation setting that were optimal for the production of images. The history of research along this line at Princeton University is told by Jack Vernon (1963). It makes a fascinating detective story; but all the leads that were obtained, and so carefully checked, were unproductive. The situational conditions responsible could not be traced. As similar difficulties were encountered by other investigators, greater attention began to be paid to conditions within the subject.

As might be expected the most satisfactory predictions are likely to be made when both sets of conditions are taken into account.

1. *Situational conditions*

There are two sets of interrelated situational variables to be discussed. The first set refers to the duration of confinement, the amount and type of visual restriction and the amount and type of movement restriction. The second class of situational variable is concerned with the instructions that are given to the subject as to what to report and how to report. No pretence is made that these are the only relevant variables, but they are the variables that have been given most attention in research so far.

(a) Duration of confinement: Contrary to the expectations of many early investigators the duration of confinement, by itself, does not appear to be a critical variable. Some subjects obtain images after 10 minutes (Ziskind and Augsburg, 1962) while others fail to report any after 2 weeks (Zubek, Welch and Saunders, 1963).

(b) Amount and type of visual restriction: Subjects have been placed in total darkness, provided with diffuse or patterned light through translucent goggles or placed within a dome reflecting homogeneous white light, but none of these conditions has been found to produce significantly more reports of imagery than another. There is, however, some evidence that total darkness may perhaps produce more of the 'meaning-less' imagery reports—flashes of light and geometrical forms (Zuckerman and Cohen, 1964).

An interesting finding by Leiderman (1960) deserves to be investigated further because it concerns the more neglected imagery modes of audition and somaesthesia. He found that visual imagery neither increased nor decreased when diffuse light was substituted for patterned light, but that somaesthetic and auditory imagery tended to increase under the greater perceptual isolation produced by diffuse light. Such a finding may be due simply to a shift in attention. If no visual infor-mation is available the subject may attend more closely to activity going on in other sense departments.

(c) Amount and type of movement restriction: Whereas it is comparatively easy to reduce stimulation impinging upon the distance receptors it is much more difficult to reduce its effect upon the somaesthetic senses of pressure, pain, temperature and kinaesthesia. Pressure and kinaesthesia are of course the most difficult to control and of these two the kinaesthetic produces the most technical difficulties. Suspension in a tank of water (e.g., Bliss and Clark, 1962) or in an iron lung (e.g., Solomon and Mendelson, 1962) has been attempted but there appears to be no simple relationship between restriction of movement and the frequency or complexity of images reported. Less severe restrictions on movement have been attempted, ranging from sitting upright on a chair to reclining at a slight angle, or lying on one's back, front or side, on a bed.

A study by Morgan and Bakan (1965) will serve as an example. They predicted that images would occur more frequently when a subject was reclining on a tilt chair than when he was sitting up. The rationale for this expectation was that sensory deprivation images . . .

. . . are dream fragments experienced in the waking state. Sleep usually occurs when lying down and is usually associated with dreams. By the mechanism of stimulus generalization, stimulus conditions similar to the sleep condition are more likely to produce dream-like experiences.

The results support the prediction, though not necessarily the theory. Whereas 12 out of 18 subjects in the reclining position reported images only 3 out of 18 subjects reported images when in the sitting position. Of 11 subjects who reported falling asleep at least once 6 came from the sitting group and 5 from the reclining.

(d) Method of reporting: Three main procedures have been utilized to obtain reports of imagery. Earlier studies reviewed by Zuckerman and Cohen (1964) showed no consistent differences in the quantity or complexity of imagery reported. A more recent study by Morgan and Bakan (1965) attempted to compare the effects of these three procedures. Three groups of twelve subjects each took part in a 1-hour isolation session. The subjects in one group were required to be silent throughout and to report their imagery afterwards (delay). The subjects in the second group were allowed to report from time to time throughout the hour (voluntary); while the members of the third group were asked to talk continuously throughout the hour (continuous). All subjects were also instructed not to move their bodies nor to close their eyes. Though method of report appears to have had no effect on either the frequency or the vividness of imagery, it was found that the continuous report procedure was the only condition in which not one of the subjects reported falling asleep.

2. *Subject conditions*

Three interrelated sets of subject variables will be considered. These cover general personality characteristics, specific beliefs regarding the effects of perceptual isolation and consequently expectations and anxieties about the experience, and lastly the motives for reporting an experience.

(a) General personality characteristics: The most comprehensive investigation of the personality characteristics of those who experience perceptual isolation imagery was conducted by Holt and Goldberger (1959) and Goldberger and Holt (1961). The 16 unemployed male actors used in this second study were selected from a pool of 50 who replied to an advertisement. Subjects wore halved table tennis balls over their eyes and padded earphones were placed over their ears through which a constant masking 'white' noise was heard. Each subject lay on his back on a comfortable bed for an

8-hour isolation period. He was then given a 90 minute battery of tests and interviewed regarding his subjective experiences. In most particulars this study was a replication of the earlier one (Holt and Goldberger, 1959) in which 14 male undergraduates had been studied. Of the large number of tests administered, only two measures were found to correlate with frequency of imagery in both studies. One was Paul's test of memory style and the other was Block's MMPI scale of neurotic under-control. Both of these measures were negatively correlated with imagery frequency. These two replicated findings were interpreted 'as being reflections of the *intellectual flexibility* and *emotional freedom* clusters' and may be regarded as part of what these workers called an 'adaptive reaction' to the isolation experience.

The resemblance between the personality characteristics of the more frequent imagers in this situation and those found by Foulkes, Spear and Symonds (1966) in their study of hypnagogic imagery are worth noting. Taken together these two studies provide some support for the notion that imagery is more likely to manifest itself in the person who has the most creative potential (see Barron, 1963).

In addition to these general findings two more specific characteristics have been reported:

(i) Prior history of hypnagogic imagery: It has been reported in two studies that subjects with a prior history of naturally-occurring hypnagogic imagery are more likely to experience other forms of imagination imagery. Freedman and his colleagues (1962) in a perceptual isolation study and Freedman and Marks (1965) in a photic stimulation study found a significant association.

It is of interest that voluntary daydreaming is found less often in those who experience perceptual isolation imagery. Solomon and Mendelson (1962) who obtained this result defined daydreaming as 'any voluntary thought concerning events in the past or anticipated in the future.'

(ii) Field independence: In a perceptual isolation study by Leiderman (1962) it was found that subjects who were most independent of their environment field as measured by the Gottschaldt test were most likely to experience perceptual isolation imagery. In another study by Freedman and Marks (1965) it was assumed that 'imagery under photic stimulation involves the ability to suspend one's generalized reality-orientation' and proposed the hypothesis that . . .

. . . people who, under ordinary circumstances, are relatively independent of their environment as a cognitive frame of reference (field independent) are more able to let this frame of reference slip away; and therefore, such people are likely to be productive of photic stimulation imagery.

Though the results did not entirely support this hypothesis, it was found that the total number of subjective colour responses was greater in those who were field independent.

From the discussion of field independence here and in a later section on hallucinations, it would appear that it is not a vital condition for the manifestation of imagery but is probably of more importance in determining whether imagery, if it does occur, is recognized as a subjective experience or whether it is assumed to be a reality based experience (i.e., an hallucination).

(b) Prior beliefs and expectations: The question of suggestion effects based upon prior beliefs and expectations is an important one to consider. If perceptual isolation imagery is a fairly robust phenomenon, it will be easier to investigate than if it is especially sensitive to minor variations in the demand characteristics of the situation and in the prior beliefs of the subjects.

In an unpublished doctoral dissertation by Camberari (1958 and cited by Freedman and Marks, 1965) it was found that suggestibility as measured by a battery of tests was positively correlated with frequency of imagery reports obtained during a perceptual isolation experiment. Further support for this finding was obtained in a study by Jackson and Kelly (1962). In fact these workers concluded that suggestion is a major variable responsible for reports of imagery in perceptual isolation studies.

In a study by Rossi, Sturrock and Solomon (1963) it was found that suggestions as to what subjects should expect to experience had little influence on reported frequency of imagery. However in their review of the evidence Zuckerman and Cohen (1964) concluded that suggestion may influence visual imagery, but that it is less likely to influence reports of auditory imagery.

Since this review the evidence has continued to show inconsistencies. In a study of their own Zuckerman and Cohen (1964a) could find no association between reports of perceptual isolation imagery and either actual knowledge or beliefs regarding perceptual isolation, or guessed-at expectation regarding experiences that might occur.

In a later study by Leon and Arnhoff (1965) the attempt was made to find out the effect of three different degrees of prior knowledge upon time estimation, discomfort experienced and the number of hallucinations reported. To count as a hallucination the reported experience had to have an out-thereness quality, be uncontrollable and be accepted as real, at least at first. Using these criteria it was found that the group given no information and the group given some factual knowledge were statistically indistinguishable in the number of hallucinations reported in the two-hour session. Significantly more hallucinations were reported by those who had been led to expect such phenomena.

Finally in a study by Short and Oskamp (1965) three hypotheses were tested: that reports of visual imagery and other unusual sensations would be greater in a one-hour perceptual deprivation session; in those who were given direct suggestions by the experimenter; in those who were volunteer subjects rather than non-volunteers, and in those periods of relative alertness as measured by large eye movements (EOG records) and alpha blocking (EEG records) during periods when imagery was being reported. No evidence was obtained in support of the first two hypothese but the third one was supported at a satisfactory level of confidence ($p < \cdot 05$).

That prior beliefs and expectations will alter the frequency and complexity of the images reported seems inevitable. Whether findings are positive or negative in studies like those reviewed will depend upon many other interacting conditions, including the characteristics of the sample, the duration of confinement, the degree and type of perceptual isolation, the instructions to the subjects and the criteria adopted for determining whether an image has been experienced. Little attention has been given so far to the effects of pretraining subjects. Presumably investigators fear that they may be unwarrantably influencing their subjects, but some study of the advantages and disadvantages of using experienced subjects should be undertaken. Failure to see what is there may be due to inexperience with what to look for. This problem was noted when discussing the observation of after-images. Failure to report what is seen or heard may be due also to a fear of seeming to be abnormal or odd.

(c) Motivation for reporting: Because the perceptual isolation experience often arouses anxiety some subjects appear to reduce it by reporting all the subjective experiences they can find. Other subjects appear to experience an increase in anxiety whenever they report on some subjective sensory phenomenon. Several attempts have been made to study the relationship between anxiety level and frequency or vividness of reported images.

In the Holt and Goldberger (1961) study discussed above it was found that subjects who showed intellectual flexibility and an absence of emotional disturbance reported significantly more imagery. A plausible hypothesis might be that the 'healthy' personality maintains an optimum level of sensory stimulation by producing more sensory equivalents (images), than does the less healthy personality. Evidence from the study by Foulkes, Spear and Symonds (1966) indicated that the more inflexible, authoritarian personality was less likely to report hypnagogic images. Perhaps the inability of the less healthy personality to produce sensory equivalents (images) or the fear of them when they tend to appear, may account for the heightened anxiety level.

That anxiety in the perceptual isolation setting may be reduced by increasing the level of sensory stimulation is shown in a study by Zuckerman and Haber (1965). These workers selected groups of high-and low-anxiety subjects on the basis of their GSR responses during an earlier three-hour perceptual isolation session. In a second three-hour isolation session the high-and low-anxiety subject were both given the opportunity to obtain random visual or auditory stimulation if they wanted it. The high-anxiety group sought out significantly more stimulation than the low-anxiety group.

However, the majority of studies reviewed by Zuckerman and Cohen (1964) report no significant relation between anxiety level and frequency or vividness of imagery. Negative findings were also reported by Morgan and Bakan (1965) who

related frequency and vividness of 'sensory deprivation hallucinations' to three measures of anxiety—the Taylor MAS, a
self-report measure of nervousness and a measure based upon
GSR readings taken during the experiment.

HALLUCINOGENIC DRUG IMAGERY

Though hashish, mescalin, lysergic acid diethylamide (LSD),
and psilocybin are among the best known hallucinogenic drugs,
most research until quite recently involved the use of mescalin.

In the form of peyote from the cactus plant *anhalonium
lewinii* the Aztec indians of ancient Mexico used mescalin in
their religious cermonies to induce a mystical state of consciousness. Prentiss and Morgan (1895) began the more
systematic examination of its hallucinogenic properties and
Klüver (1928a) surveyed the literature and reported on some
of his own investigations. In this earlier work and in a later
discussion, Klüver (1942), gives descriptions of the forms
reported by the mescalin-intoxicated person. Ardis and
McKellar (1956) have suggested that the content of mescalin
imagery more often contains the less meaningful geometrical
patterns and inanimate objects, in contrast with naturally
occurring hypnagogic imagery which tends to contain faces
or landscapes. If such a tendency is substantiated by later
investigations the explanation might be found in the greater
opportunity possessed by the habitual hypnagogic imager to
spontaneously construct meaningful images from the simpler
and initially meaningless patterns.

The mescalin may act on the person who does not normally
experience hypnagogic imagery by sensitizing him to the raw
data available in his optical equipment (e.g., phosphenes).
Perhaps meaningless optical events of this kind are perceived
literally in the same way as a person might perceive an ill-
defined object or event in his normal environment. On the
other hand the person who experiences spontaneous hypnagogic images and is sufficiently aware of them to admit to the
fact has had the opportunity throughout his life to play with
these experiences (faces in the fire and in the clouds as well as
in the dark) and to make them meaningful. Frequent exposure
to the figures in the Street Gestalt Completion test for example,
increases the probability of making them meaningful.

As with the perceptual isolation images discussed earlier a progression from the simple to the complex has also been reported for hallucinogenic drug images. Leuner (1963) writes:

In the initial stage of intoxication, or after a small dose, abnormally persistent and pronounced after-images, which may perhaps be associated with fading light or the movement of a shadow, appear in the darkened room at first. As the effect of the toxin increases, illusionary changes follow . . . The patterns of the wall began to wave and float streakily in the darkened room. The streaks lengthened and grew into writhing serpiginous patterns from which human features gradually emerged and gained in colour. Eventually, the subject was being stared at by distorted, mocking and impudent faces . . . If the subject closes his eyes at this stage, the most prosaic pictures in the mind gradually turn into coloured images which acquire an increasing amount of independence. Escaping control they take the form of novel autochtonous visions . . . As we approach the fully detailed scene, we see as a kind of intermediate stage, primitive and distinct pictorial elements such as geometrical figures and primordial creatures, passing across the visual field in sluggish procession, as if one drop of water was falling after another and then disappearing.

The administration of hallucinogenic drugs to subjects who are in a perceptual isolation situation or who are experiencing photic stimulation has been found to facilitate the manifestation of visual imagination images (McKellar and Simpson, 1954; Smythies, 1960).

PHOTIC STIMULATION AND PULSE CURRENT IMAGERY

It may be that any relatively slow rhythmic stimulation will induce either a trancelike state or drowsiness, which in turn may be expected to facilitate the occurrence of imagination images. Though visual and electro-tactile procedures have been used it would be of interest to study the effects of auditory and mechanico-tactile forms of rhythmic stimulation (see: Kahn, 1954).

The main research evidence for a relation between rhythmic stimulation and imagery comes from the use of the stroboscope (e.g., Costa, 1953; Smythies, 1960; Freedman and Marks, 1965; Horowitz, 1967) and from electrical impulses applied externally to the temples (Knoll and Kugler, 1959; Knoll, Kugler, Eichmeier and Höfer, 1962; Knoll and Kugler, 1964).

In these studies the usual range of meaningless and meaningful images have been reported, though the first are far more common than the second.

The only study to report personality correlates of imagery frequency is that of Freedman and Marks (1965). Visual imagery reports were coded for form and colour and the cognitive and personality measures included an embedded figures test, the Rorschach, the Barron-Welsh art scale and an imagery and creativity questionnaire.

During the photic stimulation sessions the subjects reclined on a bed with eyes closed, in a dark room. In the 'spontaneous reporting condition' the stroboscope was placed 1 inch from the subject's nose to ensure that the entire visual field was covered. Each exposure to the flashing light lasted 10 seconds and progressed from a frequency of 1 flash a second at the first exposure up to 20 flashes a second at the last. In a second 'suggestion condition' exposures were increased to 30-second periods and the rate of flash fixed at 15 a second. Subjects were again asked to describe everything they saw but to watch out for such forms as circles, squares, spirals, stars, flowers, animals and people.

In general these workers obtained results which are consistent with those of Holt and Goldberger (1959), Goldberger and Holt (1961) and Foulkes, Spear and Symonds (1966) "that an artistic, sensitive and creative self concept is related to a syndrome that includes imagery". In particular, a prior history of naturally occurring hypnagogic imagery, emotional responsiveness to external stimuli (Rorschach colour sum ratio), and self ratings on imaginative ability (though not objective tests of it), were all found to be related to visual imagery produced by rhythmic photic stimulation.

In a study of pulse current imagery reported by Knoll *et al* (1962) it was found that more or less shapeless flicker effects were produced in all 150 subjects when pulse currents between 5 and 100 c.p.s., between 0.5 and 3.5 volts, and between 0.1 and 1.4 milli-amperes were applied to the forehead through flannel-coated silver electrodes (6 x 4 cms.). Forty-six of the 150 subjects experienced shaped light patterns. This proportion of about one third is essentially the same as that obtained by Leaning (1926) and by McKellar and Simpson (1954) for naturally occurring hypnagogic imagery. In another paper

Knoll and Kugler (1959) have reported that the particular forms obtained are a function of the frequency of the low voltage square wave potentials that are used as stimuli. It was also found that these 'subjective light patterns' were most readily observed when the eyes were closed and dark adapted.

Hallucinations

It has already been noted that some students of perceptual isolation imagery have used the term hallucination in its technically correct sense. However, it is not always clear whether a subject must believe in the objective reality of his perceptual experience for a few minutes or for some indefinite length of time for the experience to be classified as an hallucination. When the subject, reported by Freedman and his colleagues, 'tried to eat an "imaged" salad' he presumably recognized the error of his perception soon afterwards. When a person continues to act as if he believed in his projected image, even after having been shown that it must be false, we speak of him as deluded. Yet we would not want to say that true hallucinations only occur in those who have a pre-existing delusion.

Perhaps, after all, it makes most sense to speak of an hallucination as a percept-like experience, whose objective reality is assumed without question. In the normal person a realization that an image has been confused with a percept will occur more or less quickly depending upon such factors as the motivation and the opportunity to check upon the experience.

If the person has a delusion into which the experience can be fitted the motivation to check will be absent. If the person with a delusion is forced to resolve the dissonance between his experience and an objective demonstration of its falsity, he is most likely to provide a rationalization that will permit a continued belief in his delusion.

A somewhat similar situation exists for the relatively normal person who believes in ghosts. Many of the meaningful subjective experiences described in this chapter may very easily be interpreted as apparitions. The percept-like experience is recognized as non-material, but is not recognized as being a subjective phenomenon. The 'ghost' is perceived within a reference frame which includes the possibility of apparitions.

The problem to be considered in this section is concerned with the factors that make it more or less likely that an individual will confuse an image with a percept or in more general terms, will confuse fantasy with reality.

A useful way to think about this problem is to use the concept of conceptual boundaries (Goldstone, 1962). One such boundary is the body image boundary discussed by Fisher (1962). He points out that those who find it difficult . . .

. . . to demarcate one's body bounds from what is 'out there' is presumed to confuse the whole process of stimulus identification and localization and to result eventually in an inability to discriminate whether experiences represent inside of the body or outside of the body events.

Fisher then proceeds to quote investigations that quite 'specifically pinpoint boundary loss as a factor in the development of hallucinations' in schizophrenics, and in the phantom limb experiences of amputees.

The field dependence-independence dimension may reasonably be interpreted in terms of the related concept of perceptual boundaries. The field-dependent person is more susceptible to the influence of context than is the field-independent person. He finds it more difficult to make accurate judgments of the gravitational uprightness of a rod when the sides of the frame within which it is placed deviate from the vertical. Again, the field-dependent person is less able to ignore the distracting lines surrounding a pattern in the Hidden Figures Test; the perceptual boundaries are easily destroyed. In this regard, delusional subjects may be expected to show more rigid conceptual boundaries than non-delusional subjects and should therefore be less field-dependent. Taylor (1956) obtained evidence in support of this hypothesis. He compared a sample of male psychotics, delusions only, with a sample of male psychotics who were not deluded but who experienced hallucinations.

The latter group was more field-dependent than the former. In a perceptual isolation study in which normal subjects were used, Holt and Goldberger (1959) found no difference in the frequency with which images were reported by field independent and field dependent subjects, but field dependent subjects were more likely to attribute their imagery to an 'outside' source.

Further support for the conceptual boundaries concept is provided in a study by Silverman (1961) and his colleagues. From a sample of 109 students the 9 most field-independent and the 11 most field-dependent were selected to take part in a two-hour perceptual isolation experiment. Of the field-dependent subjects, 4 reported meaningful visual imagery to which they gave reality status while none of the field-independent subjects reported this type of imagery.

Another line of evidence on the significance of the conceptual boundary concept is provided by Goldstone's (1962) research on intersensory differences. He found that in normal subject . . .

. . . auditory and visual time judgments are markedly different from each other such that significantly more visual than auditory clock time is necessary to account for the same temporal concept. This intersensory difference was not found with the patient group, providing evidence that this population may be less able to differentiate among senses and conceptually define intersensory distinctions. In summary, it is felt that hallucinatory experence can be accounted for in part by increased reduction in the conceptual intersensory boundaries.

If it could be shown that hallucinators are less familiar with the experience of having an image, then it might be argued that the specific perceptual confusion could result from an individual's assumption that if something is seen or heard the probability is high that an external correlate for the experience exists. In fact one might put forward the tentative hypothesis that reports of ordinary memory imagery are relatively weak in those who hallucinate.

Evidence in support of this hypothesis will be presented in a moment, but it is of interest to note that the exact opposite of this hypothesis was often asserted in the past. For example, Sully (1905) expressed the prevailing psychiatric views of his time when he wrote: 'The hallucinations of insanity are due to a projection of mental images which have, owing to certain circumstances, gained a preternatural persistence and vividness.'

Before attempting to test this nineteenth century notion, Seitz and Molholm (1947) carried out a review of the literature. Only four previous studies could be found, all of which had given negative results, but all of which suffered from a variety of inadequacies in terms of sample size and method of measuring imagery with schizophrenic subjects. Seitz and Molholm administered the Griffitts (1924) test of concrete imagery to three groups. In the first group were 40 schizophrenics, 20 of whom were known to experience auditory hallucinations while the remaining 20 were known not to experience hallucinations. In the second group were 10 patients who had recently recovered from alcoholic hallucinosis and who were awaiting discharge. The third group was a normal one consisting of 114 student nurses. All the patients were tested individually, but the student nurses were tested under conditions of group administration. The authors report that:

Schizophrenic patients with auditory hallucinations were found to have a significantly lower mean percentage of auditory imagery than either normal subjects or schizophrenic patients without auditory hallucinations. The normal subjects and the schizophrenic patients without auditory hallucinations did not differ significantly in this respect. Patients who had recovered from alcoholic hallucinosis were found to have a significantly lower mean percentage of auditory imagery than normal subjects. The mean percentage of auditory imagery for patients who had recovered from an alcoholic hallucinosis and for schizophrenic patients with auditory hallucinations did not differ significantly.

In conclusion they suggested 'that one of the factors responsible for auditory hallucinations is relatively deficient auditory imagery'. Further support for this association between subjective reports of poor imagery and predisposition to experience hallucinations is to be found in a study by Thale (1950) and his colleagues, who investigated the effect of mescalin upon visual imagination images. The subjects took a test of memory imagery before the administration of mescalin. From their findings the authors concluded that the evidence was very strong 'that a low imagery score predisposes to hallucination'.

In a study by MacIndoe and Singer (1966) it was hypothesized that: 'psychotic groups of spontaneous hallucinators will image so vividly that after effects will occur.' However, as might be expected from the findings already reported, the results showed that the hallucinators were no better than the non-hallucinators in producing after-effects to an imaged stimulus.

Finally, in a study of the Perky effect with a sample of normal university students, Segal and Nathan (1964) report . . .

. . . a tendency for Ss who are 'easy' imagers to identify the Perky experience as a perception at relatively low levels of intensity. That is, it appears that Ss who are familiar with their internal experiences, who can produce images easily are well able to distinguish these images from reality.

Among the further tests that might be made of this latter hypothesis is the comparison of a sample of visualizers with a sample of verbalizers under the conditions used to produce the Perky effect. Even more clear-cut results should be obtained than those reported above by Segal and Nathan (1964). Segal (1964) reported that subjects who tended to misidentify the stimulus as part of their own imagery were more likely to be field-dependent as measured by scores on the Embedded Figures Test and the Stroop colour word test. They were also found to be less familiar with their inner world of subjective experience as measured on some of the subscales of the As (1962) questionnaire of subjective personal experiences.

A comment on the way in which Seitz and Molholm (1947) and Thale and his co-workers (1950) have interpreted their results is now desirable. Their results are interpreted as showing that weak imagery is 'responsible for' or 'predisposes to' the occurrence of hallucinations. In the light of the evidence cited here it seems more likely that both weak imagery, as measured by self-report techniques, and the occurrence of hallucinatory experiences, result from a lack of familiarity with the internal stimulus environment.

Mention of self-report techniques in this context raises an important question. Are self-report tests of voluntary imagery vividness any more than general measures of responsiveness to one's internal environment? In a factor analytic study of daydreaming by Singer and Antrobus (1963) seven major factors (styles of daydreaming) emerged. One of these was called 'enjoyment of daydreaming' and is defined by items which imply that the internal environment is accepted, enjoyed and used. How would scores on this subscale correlate with scores on a self-report test of imagery vividness? How would it mediate predictions of the kind made in relation to vividness of voluntary imagery?

The material reviewed in this section suggests that visual hallucinations are more likely to occur in persons who have vivid imagination images, but who lack any general ability to differentiate an inner world of quasi-sensory events from an outer world of genuine sensory events. Perhaps the main reason why weak imagery has been found in association with hallucinations is due to the self-report method of measuring imagery, and not to an absence of vivid imagery; after all, an hallucination *is* a vivid imagination image.

Research on the body image boundary concept also suggests that hallucinators are unable to differentiate between sensory events that arise within the body and sensory events that arise outside the boundaries of one's body. One very interesting study (McGuigan, 1966) which presents evidence congruent with this view, also indicates that the voices heard in an auditory hallucination may result from the sub-audible speech of the patient himself. Muscle action potentials (MAP) were obtained from chin and tongue as well as from a control area on the left forearm. Pneumographic recordings were taken from the chest and abdomen while overt verbalizations were recorded via a microphone fixed about three inches in front of the mouth. The psychotic subject used in this experiment was asked to press a button every time he heard his voices and then to repeat aloud what they had said. McGuigan concluded that: 'at least in one psychotic S, covert oral language behaviour occurred significantly often before, and immediately prior to, the report of an auditory hallucination.'

Discussion and Conclusions

As in many areas of science, two basic approaches to the classification of data are found. Some workers emphasize similarities while others emphasize differences—the lumpers and the splitters.

Preference for one or other of these approaches is in part a function of individual personality and in part a function of the state of knowledge at a particular time. Both these factors have influenced the lumping approach that has been adopted here. The facts suggest that a broad conceptual framework is not intrinsically absurd and that the attempt to construct such a framework might encourage more research aimed at supporting or refuting it.

In presenting this framework, the first section is concerned with the two basic conditions necessary for the occurrence of imagination imagery. In the second section the part played by the spontaneous activity of the sensory apparatus will be considered in relation to past learning and present motivation.

This chapter will be concluded with a brief discussion on the significance of imagination imagery for the study of creativity.

A FRAMEWORK FOR UNDERSTANDING IMAGINATION IMAGERY

1. *Attending to the inner world*

The probability that a person will become aware of and attend to an inner world of stimulus events is increased when he remains awake and when all external stimuli have ceased to be functionally operative.

This is the essence of West's (1962) 'perceptual release theory of hallucinations'. He believes that what normally prevents the emergence of images into consciousness is the presence of varied sensory input from our environment:

When effective (attention-commanding) sensory input decreases below a certain threshold, there may be a release into awareness of previously recorded perceptions through the disinhibition of the brain circuits that represent them. If a general level of cortical arousal persists to a sufficient degree, these released perceptions can enter awareness and be experienced as hallucinations. The greater the level of arousal, the more vivid the hallucinations.

Though the implication in West's theory is that the 'hallucinations' (imagination images) are a centrally determined phenomenon, it will be proposed a little later that peripheral elements may also be involved. The interest of West's theory in the present context is that it provides a pair of conditions that are common to all the procedures known to induce imagination imagery. Naturally occurring hypnagogic imagery by definition involves the presence of reduced sensory stimulation and some degree of conscious awareness. The effect of hallucinogenic drugs may be attributed to their two-way action as 'sensory poisons and diencephalic stimulants' (West, 1962). Rhythmic photic stimulation and pulse currents applied externally both produce a mild trance state in which awareness of other sensory input is reduced. Meditation (Pinard, 1957) reduces awareness of all distracting sensory processes while maintaining a high level of arousal in relation to the object of contemplation. In a comparison of imagination images occurring in hallucinations and pseudo hallucinations with those occurring in phantom limb phenomena, Bartlett (1951) notes that both experiences occur 'in the absence of normal stimuli to the part of the brain concerned'. He points out that the phantom is more likely to disappear when an artificial limb is worn, or when the stump is subjected to pressure or repeated percussion.

All forms of perceptual isolation would appear to act in the same way, but in this, as in the other procedures for producing the two conditions under discussion, it has become abundantly clear that individual susceptibility to the experience of imagery varies greatly. It will now be appropriate to consider these variations in individual susceptibility.

2. *Variations in susceptibility to imagination imagery*

These variations will be considered first, as they occur within the sensory apparatus itself, second, within the past learning experience of the subject and third, as they occur within the context of present motivation.

(a) Variations in the sensory apparatus: Workers in all the areas of imagination imagery have remarked upon the reports of meaningless subjective visual experiences. What has become increasingly clear is that these 'form constants' as Klüver (1928a, 1942) called them may serve as the sensory core around which many imagination images are elaborated. Careful descriptions of these form constants have been given by Klüver (1928a) in relation to a wide range of stimulus conditions. More specific descriptions have been given by Leaning (1926) for hypnagogic imagery; Smythies (1959, 1960) for photic stimulation imagery; Pinard (1957) for meditation imagery; Knoll and Kugler (1964) and Kellogg, Knoll and Kugler (1965) for pulse current imagery; Hebb (1954) for perceptual isolation imagery; and Horowitz (1964) for schizophrenic hallucinations and the everyday experiences of many normal subjects. These form constants consist of 'self-luminous geo-metrical or abstract patterns such as arcs, circles, wheels, stars, waves, stripes, multiples of dots, squares, spirals, lattice structures or triangles' (Knoll and Kugler, 1964). Drawings of these various structures are available in Smythies (1959, 1960), Knoll, Kugler, Eichmeier and Höfer (1962) and Horowitz (1964). It has been suggested by Horowitz that the two entopic sources of these forms are probably the retinal ganglionic network and the anatomic bodies within the eyeball itself. The retinal ganglionic network is connected on the input side with the rods and cones and on the output side with the optic nerve.

The anatomic bodies within the eye are also sufficiently varied to account for the form constants. The following description is provided by Horowitz (1964).

The patterns of the retinal blood vessels affect the light-sensitive rods and cones peripheral to the macula lutea, the area of precise vision. The shadows of such vessels could give rise to the wavy, radiating, filigreed elements; the blood cells within them might produce dot-like apparitions. The optic disc, i.e., the central scotoma, could give rise to the large circular figures and the layers of rods, cones and neural bundles to the parallel figures. The fibres of the lens are arranged around six diverging axes; this causes the rays seen around distant lights (giving them a star-like lustre) and can also produce a sense of parallel fibres, swirls or spots when such defects are present. The muscae volitantes, or floaters in the vitreous humor, like the artifacts in the lens, are produced by the invagination of integument during embryonal development of the eye and can give rise to oval or irregular shapes in entoptic visions. The movement of dots could be the flow of formed blood elements. The constant variations in optic movement caused by tremor, flicker and drift would also impart a sense of movement to the elements.

Clearly, there is enough going on within the eye to provide the basis for a full length Hollywood spectacular. Is there any evidence that these 'entoptic glimmerings' as Havelock Ellis (1911) once called them are ever, in fact, used as the basis of imagination imagery.

Ladd (1892) cites Johannes Müller as having written in 1826 on this particular problem: 'I often follow these appearances for a half-hour, until they finally pass over into the dream images of sleep.'

The opposite process, in which dream images dissolve into their entoptic components, is described by Ladd (1892). He writes:

Almost without exception, when I am able to recall the visual images of my dream and to observe the character of the retinal field quickly enough to compare the two, the schemata of the luminous and coloured retinal phantasms afford the undoubted clue to the origins of the things just seen in my dream life.

More recently Horowitz (1964) carefully questioned a number of hallucinating schizophrenics and concluded: 'Descriptions that sounded as though the hallucination had exfoliated from a simple form were so common, however, that a hypothesis of some optic phenomenon providing the nidus for such elaborations was formed.'

Among the modern writers on hypnagogic imagery McKellar and Simpson (1954), a similar account has been given.

Hypnagogic imagery, we suggest, does not take place against a screen of darkness, but against a changing screen of patterns and colours on to which the central processes are projected . . . The outline of the images is provided by the luminous dust, but these are interpreted on the basis of such past perceptions as are reactivated.

However, it should be remarked that many of the simple meaningless forms, of the kind described here, have also been produced by direct electrical stimulation of the exposed occipital cortex (Penfield, 1952). That these simple meaningless forms might also result from the 'activation of preformed neurone networks in the visual system' has been suggested by Kellogg, Knoll and Kugler (1965). These workers cite some preliminary evidence to suggest that the maturation of some neurological structures within the visual system ('neurone chain oscillators or coincident filters with small band width within the EEG frequency range') may underlie the emergence of geometric scribble patterns in three-to four-year old children as well as the phosphene forms observed by adults. Children do not scribble a wide range of patterns 'but only a limited number of "basic" ones' which correspond to the basic phosphene forms found in adults.

(b) Variations in past learning: It has been mentioned on several occasions that most people remain unaware of their imagery, even of their after-imagery, because they have learned to ignore it. It is a distraction if it is noticed and it has no positive value in most of the practical activities of life. For these reasons it is not surprising that the threshold for the perception of imagination imagery will be high in many people, at least initially. If in addition the individual feels anxious when vivid autonomous visual or other images are experienced, the defence of selective inattention may well be learned. It is possible that when imagery *is* experienced by someone who is either unfamiliar with it or defensively protected against it, that a reality status is more likely to be attributed to it.

A second relevant aspect of past learning is whether the individual emphasizes literalness in his perception or meaningful organization. If he is inclined to be a literal perceiver and he experiences an entoptic event, it is more likely to be seen as a meaningless image. In the same way the literal perceiver would be less likely to see anything in a cloud, live coals, or an inkblot, other than the cloud, coal or blot itself.

(c) Variation in present motivation: Though current motivations may be expected to influence the probability of having an imagination image, the present concern is with its effect upon the content of what is experienced. As is well known, the content of an hallucination typically reveals some aspects of the patients' anxieties or conflicts, just as dreams may do. Imagery, as Fromm (1952) has observed, is something of a 'forgotten language' but it is nevertheless a remarkably important internal one for the representation of problems and their solutions. For this reason imagination imagery plays a prominent part in the creative activity of artists in all media (Ghiselin, 1952; McKellar, 1957, 1963; Oster, 1966; Tauber and Green, 1959).

One of the most detailed accounts of the way in which motivational states influence the content of an imagination image is provided by Silberer (1951). As early as 1909 he wrote:

In a state of drowsiness I contemplate an abstract topic such as the nature of trans-subjectively (for all people) valid judgments. A struggle between active thinking and drowsiness sets in. The latter becomes strong enough to disrupt normal thinking and to allow— in the twilight state so produced—the appearance of an auto-symbolic phenomenon. The content of my thought presents itself to me immediately in the form of a perceptual (for an instant apparently real) picture. I see a big circle (or transparent sphere) in the air with people around it whose heads reach into the circle. This symbol expresses practically everything I was thinking of. The trans-subjective judgment is valid for all people without exception: the circle includes all the heads. The validity must have its grounds in a commonality: the heads belong all in the same homogeneous sphere. Not all judgments are trans-subjective: the body and limbs of the people are outside (below) the sphere as they stand on the ground as independent individuals. In the next instant (I did not go to sleep) I realize that it is a dream picture; the thought that gave rise to it, which I had forgotten for the moment, now comes back and I recognize the experience as an 'autosymbolic' phenomenon. What had happened? In my drowsiness my abstract ideas were, without my conscious interference, replaced by a perceptual picture —by a symbol. My abstract chain of thoughts was hampered; I was too tired to go on thinking in that form; the perceptual picture emerged as an 'easier' form of thought. It afforded an appreciable relief, comparable to the one experienced when sitting down after a strenuous walk. It appears to follow—as a corollary—that such 'picture-thinking' requires less effort than the usual kind.

In Werner and Kaplan's (1963) discussion of cognitive development in children, image thinking is postulated as one of the earliest stages. Though it is impossible to get direct evidence to test this hypothesis with children, indirect evidence is cited from experiments similar to those of Silberer. In the struggle to give form to an idea, imagery provides one of the easiest means of representing it and this can be demonstrated in adults. It is not merely a physical object that can be represented in visual imagery but almost any subtlety of logical relationships. For example, adult subjects were asked to represent in imaged form a set of conjunctional sentences that differed only in the conjunction used, e.g.:

He is intelligent *because* he is cautious.
He is intelligent *but* he is cautious.

It was found that the images which developed to represent these and other types of logical relation were very similar to those found in dreams. For example, one subject represented 'He is intelligent *because* he is cautious' with an image of: 'a girl with her books; at the same time she's smiling, she's neat, her mouth is closed, and I see her walking around a puddle'.

These images have the spontaneity and originality of the imagination image discussed elsewhere in this chapter though they may sometimes lack some of the vividness and out-thereness.

Similar experiments to those of Werner and Kaplan (1963) are required, in which the essential conditions of reduced sensory stimulation and relative alertness are produced. It might be hypothesized that in a person capable of producing imagination imagery such sentences would crystallize even more readily' into an appropriate symbolic image. The significance of such studies for problem-solving is potentially very great. What is not immediately available as a verbalized thought may appear as a symbolic pictorial image. Though this process is commonplace in nocturnal dreams and is often used to gain insight into personal problems it has been studied very little in the context of waking thought and of impersonal problems.

IMAGINATION IMAGERY AND CREATIVITY

Quite apart from the overtones of meaning in the term 'imagination-image', the anecdotal literature on creativity is full of examples of the way in which artists and scientists have used their spontaneously occurring imagination-images (e.g., Ghiselin, 1952). After the preparation and incubation phases (Wallis, 1926) the illumination phase often takes the form of a vivid visual image which represents directly or symbolically the solution sought. An ever-popular example of this is provided by the concept of the benzene ring which was 'revealed' to Professor Kekulé in an hypnagogic state.

Sometimes imagination imagery provides the painter or writer with the essential idea for a picture or a poem. William Blake and Samuel Coleridge are two classic examples, but an interesting contemporary one is provided by the cinematographic imagery of Enid Blyton. In a letter to PeterMcKellar she describes the way in which ideas for her Noddy stories occur.

I shut my eyes for a few minutes, with my portable typewriter on my knee. I make my mind a blank and wait—and then, as clearly as I would see real children, my characters stand before me in my mind's eye . . . The story is enacted almost as if I had a private cinema screen there . . . I don't know what is going to happen. I am in the happy position of being able to write a story and read it for the first time at one and the same moment . . . Sometimes a character makes a joke, a really funny one that makes me laugh as I type it on my paper and I think 'Well, I couldn't have thought of that myself in a hundred years!' and then I think: 'Well who *did* think of it?' (McKellar, 1957).

Little research has been undertaken so far to investigate the process and products of creativity under conditions associated with imagination imagery. Of the two studies known to the writer, the first employed perceptual isolation and the second used an hallucinogenic drug. Philip Kubzansky (1961) found that the number, clarity and complexity of visual images experienced during a two and one-half hour perceptual isolation period were correlated with scores on a previously administered battery of Guildford pencil and paper tests of creativity.

In a pilot study on the relation of LSD to creative problem solving, Harman and his co-workers (1966) found that eleven different conditions believed to be important to the process of achieving novel and effective problem solutions were all facilitated during the drug session. One of these conditions was the possession of a high capacity for visual imagery and fantasy. A typical comment from one subject who was trying to solve a problem in circuit design suggests the utility of heightened imaging ability.

I began to see an image of the circuit. The gates themselves were little silver cones linked together by lines. I watched this circuit flipping through its paces . . . The psychedelic state, is for me at least, an immensely powerful one for obtaining insight and understanding through visual symbolism.

The subjects of this study were all concerned with problem solving in their professional work. A high proportion of the problem solutions attained during the LSD session, were found to work satisfactorily when verification was undertaken in the weeks that followed.

Chapter 6

CONCLUSIONS AND SPECULATIONS

THE separation of imagery into four classes is a convenient but somewhat arbitrary procedure. It is convenient because it has made it possible to focus on some characteristics of imagery that would not otherwise stand out so clearly in discussion. It is arbitrary because so much of the phenomenal experience is similar for each class, though no one knows to what extent imagery of one class is related to imagery of another.

In so far as the phenomenal attributes of one class typically differ from those of another, they do so, chiefly, on the dimension of vividness and controllability. Apart from individual differences in regard to each of these dimensions, each class of imagery tends to be consistently more or less vivid and more or less controllable.

Thus, after imagery is *relatively vivid* but *impossible to control*. While the after-effects of the original stimulus are still operative within the sense organ, the after-image emerges into awareness with almost the same imperious insistence as a present sensation. Eidetic imagery, which is dependent upon the stimulus to a slightly lesser extent may be characterized as *relatively vivid* but subject to somewhat *more control* than the after-image. Because of the after-effects following exposure to a stimulus the immediate appearance of this eidetic-image may resemble the after-image more than it does when reconstructed on some later occasion. When reconstructed some days or weeks later it may be found that it is more like a vivid memory-image. It is possible that the interval between original stimulation and recall could account for the difference between the views of Allport (1924) and Morsh and Abbott (1945). While Allport had suggested that eidetic imagery is essentially a variety of memory imagery, Morsh and Abbott asserted that it was essentially a variety of after-imagery.

Ordinary memory imagery involves the reconstruction of a past percept and is to this extent a more centrally initiated event, not dependent upon the persistence of sensory after-effects. It is characteristically *less vivid* and *more controllable* than either the after image or the immediate eidetic image.

Lastly comes the imagination image which is as vivid, if not *more vivid*, than an eidetic image, but whereas some individuals can exercise control over their eidetic images it is typically found that the imagination image is *less controllable*. It is of central origin but it is possible that some of its vividness and lack of controllability is due to the spontaneous and ambiguous events occurring in the sense organs themselves (e.g., 'floaters' in the eye).

The foregoing account indicates that the experience of becoming aware of a particular class of imagery varies, more or less, on a continuum which extends from almost complete determination by the persistence of a stimulus in the relevant sensory receptor to almost complete determination by events that are centrally initiated.

With practice almost anyone can become aware of his after-images. Is there any reason to believe that this is not also true of the other classes of imagery? Though the evidence suggests that eidetic imagery may involve some special ability or disability, it is probably true that the capacity to experience memory and imagination images is universal. This does not mean, of course, that there may not be rare persons who lack this capacity, just as there are rare persons who lack other basic capacities (e.g., the capacity to feel pain; Cohen and his associates, 1955). Nevertheless, the evidence from modern dream research shows that lack of capacity to image is indeed rare. Even those who have always believed themselves to be non-dreamers report visual dreams when awakened from a period of EEG Stage I, REM sleep (e.g., Goodenough and his associates, 1959). As all dreaming involves the presence of images and as all people probably dream, at least this form of imaging would appear to be a common *human capacity*. It is not, however, a common *human ability*, and training may even be necessary for some people before they became aware of their after-images. With memory images, as many as 10 % of an educated, adult population believe themselves to be totally lacking in ability to experience them (McKellar, 1963). As for imagination imagery, at least in the form of naturally occurring hypnagogic imagery, as many as 66 % of an adult population may report that they can recall no occasion on which one such image has been experienced. Failure to become aware of imagery is due chiefly to inattention to, and consequent lack of familiarity with, internal channels of stimulation. One method of training subjects to become aware of their imagery is suggested from the results of a study on alpha rhythm control by Kamiya and Zeitlin (1963). Subjects lay in a darkened, sound-deadened room with eyes closed. They were told that two states of mind existed and that these were associated with the presence and absence of alpha waves. Their task was to discover which state of mind produced a suppression of alpha.

The design of the study was like that of an instrumental conditioning experiment. When alpha waves appeared and persisted for at least two or three cycles the subject was informed by intercom that a 30-second conditioning trial had begun. A 400 c.p.s. tone at 30 db above threshold was then sounded and remained on for the full period of the trial, except for periods when the alpha rhythm disappeared. On these occasions the tone ceased and provided an opportunity for the subject to discriminate between his state of mind when the tone was on and his state of mind when the tone was absent. At the end of each 30-second trial the subject was again informed by intercom. The inter-trial interval was approximately 15 seconds with about 10 trials to a block. During the inter-block intervals, of between 2 and 5 minutes, the subject was asked to describe what he believed to be the relevant mental activities associated with those periods of a trial when the tone was turned off. The inter-block interval was also used to obtain samples of a subject's basal alpha amplitude.

Most subjects in the experiment learned to control their alpha rhythm and learned that the self-produced controlling stimulus was some form of visual imagery. One subject described the method by which he was able to cause the tone to cease (i.e., produce alpha blocking): 'The tone seems to be a function of non-verbal thought . . . I just picture the object.' Another said: 'I avoid just saying words, and instead see the picture in front of me.'

The evidence seemed to show that the subjects had learned to use the inner cue of imagery as a means of controlling their alpha rhythm. A check was made to discover whether heart rate, respiration pattern, eye movements or muscle tension changes were correlated with changes in alpha rhythm, but no correlations were found and it was concluded that these potential cues could not be responsible for the learning that had occurred.

The significance of this procedure in the present context is simply to show one way in which a 'non-visualizer' might be aided to become aware of his latent imagery, but its significance goes far beyond this immediate purpose. If a subject can gain control of his own alpha rhythm why should he not be able to gain control of other EEG rhythms or physiological states associated with other known psychological conditions. If the EEG patterns associated with the subjective states of Zen meditation can be clearly established, then instrumental conditioning procedures like those of Dr. Kamiya might be used to shape up the internal responses that sustain the appropriate EEG pattern and thereby produce the actual state of meditation. Perhaps insomniacs could learn to induce sleep in this way or hypertensive persons learn to reduce their blood pressure. The procedure outlined above appears to be one of a general class of procedures called 'coverant control' by Homme (1965). The term 'coverant' is a contraction of 'covert operant'. Just as an operant is a response that brings about some change in the external environment, so a coverant is one that brings about some change in the internal environment. By arranging that the emitted response (coverant), e.g., muscle relaxation or daydreaming, is positively reinforced then these forms of behaviour can be brought under the control of the contingency manager. The contingency manager (controller of reinforcement possibilities) may be another or it may be oneself. Learning to discriminate the desired coverant from the non-desired coverant, e.g., discriminating the state of relaxing from the state of tensing, may be a necessary first step.

From what has been said above it seems highly probable that the frequency and perhaps the vividness and controllability of imagery in 'non-visualizers' could be increased. More experimental work along the lines already suggested by Kamiya and Zeitlin, and implied in the work of Homme, is now necessary.

Whatever the outcome in terms of the possibility of modifying the covert behaviour of imaging, individual differences in the habitual use of imagery or its habitual non-use appear to have some potential for an understanding of other cognitive activities. Some of the ways in which the significance of imagery may manifest itself have been suggested at many places in the last four chapters. In the remaining pages of this final chapter the significance of imaging will be considered as it relates to, or manifest itself in, other cognitive and motivational processes. Altogether four questions have been asked by way of producing an orientation to significant groups of problems.

1. *How do perceptual achievements, such as those involved in responding to an ambiguous ink blot or in recognition of an object, differ for individuals who are classified as habitual visualizers and habitual verbalizers?* In considering this problem it is necessary to re-emphasize that the classification of individuals into habitual visualizers and habitual verbalizers is to some extent arbitrary, both in terms of cut-off points and in terms of the measures used. Habitual visualizers may on occasion resort to inner speech and may engage in problem solving without being aware of any accompanying imagery. Nevertheless, visual imagery is a frequent and spontaneous accompaniment to much of their thinking and to most of their day dreaming. Visual images arise easily and may be utilized deliberately as a method of concretely representing some past, present or future event. The presence of imagery gives confidence when an habitual visualizer is engaged in any mental task, but its presence does not guarantee accuracy and in difficult tasks involving abstraction it may even impede progress towards a successful solution.

At another level of thought are the habitual verbalizers, some of whom may know what it is like to experience a fleeting memory image, but for none does the visual image have a significant part to play in their mental life. Problem solving is often an imageless process, though it may be accompanied by larger or lesser amounts of inner speech.

Both concrete imagery and inner speech can serve as cues or markers so that in reflecting upon a problem the thinker gets a feeling of recognition. For example, when taking up a problem after an interval engaged in some other activity one quickly recognizes that a particular train of images or an internal monologue occurred before and at a particular point in the thought sequence.

The issue of what part the phenomenal experience of an image might play in perception or in problem solving is not part of this question but will be taken up later. The present question is essentially concerned with the differential effects of a particular cognitive style upon the achievement of a perceptual response. That these two cognitive styles might be important moderator variables in perceptual experiments was suggested in an earlier chapter. Before describing any recent studies in which they have been employed some early findings by Bartlett (1932) will be discussed.

When Bartlett began his celebrated series of cognitive experiments over fifty years ago he reported on an individual difference variable which appears to be essentially the same as the one now under consideration. He talked about the tendency towards visualizing or vocalizing in different subjects faced with the same cognitive task. When the task consisted in looking at a series of inkblots in an effort to report what they reminded him of, responses varied enormously, but those of his subjects whom Bartlett came to regard as primarily visualizers, produced characteristically different responses from those of the verbalizers.

For the visualizer, inspection of a blot would often evoke an affective response first, followed fairly quickly by a richly detailed account of a particular concrete personal memory. The vocalizers had slower reaction times and tended to adopt a problem solving attitude to the task. Responses were less marked by the presence of feeling and were not personal or concrete in their content. Some vocalizers found it difficult or impossible to produce responses to all thirteen blots, and even when responses were given they usually had reference to a general class of object or events and not to particular instances. Some examples of the typical responses produced by vocalizers are the following: butterfly, bird, child walking, footmarks, Isle of Skye.

In a more recent study by Drewes (1958) visualizers and non-visualizers were selected on the basis of alpha rhythm criteria (see Table 4.3 on p. 69) and their responses to the ten cards of the Rorschach were then compared. The results were similar to those obtained in the Bartlett study. Whereas the visualizers produced signficantly more realistically integrated responses involving combinations of form and colour (FC), significantly more responses involving the integration of the whole blot (W) the non-visualizers (verbalizers?) produced 'easier' responses lacking concrete detail. In fact, the non-visualizers produced significantly more responses having a diffuse tactile quality (cF +c), significantly more vague responses like clouds or smoke (K) and significantely more responses in which animals were seen in movement (FM). Visualizers also produced more responses (R) than non-visualizers.

As in the Bartlett study these results suggest that non-visualizers are more likely to adopt a problem solving approach to the task of finding something meaningful in an inkblot. They tend to stay close to the blot in the sense of searching out the more 'obvious' structures that appear there. To say that a blot looks like 'a fleece' (cF) or like 'clouds' (K) is to give back a visual synonym, i.e., a response which is little more than a restatement of the blot's essential ambiguity. To say that a blot or a part of it looks like a 'map' (F) or a 'climbing animal' (FM) is to stay close to the bare shape of it. Such responses do not go beyond classifying into fairly general categories, whereas the visualizer produces responses which integrate concrete personal content with the objective features of the blot.

In both the studies reported so far the task has involved making sense out of an objectively meaningless stimulus, and the evidence suggests that visualizers can integrate more qualities of a blot to produce a highly particularized response. What happens when the task is changed and the visualizer knows that an objectively correct response is required and possible? Such a situation exists in a recognition task where the object to be identified is presented with varying degrees of ambiguity. Frederiksen (1965) measured speed of recognition by noting the focus stage (on a 15-point scale from blurred to clear) at which each of twenty colour slide pictures was accurately identified. Of the five cognitive factors investigated only visualization showed a consistent correlation (negative) with speed of recognition. Visualization as measured in this study was discussed in chapter four under the heading of 'visualizing efficiency'. The measure used was the one defined by French and his colleagues (1963) as the 'ability to manipulate or transform the image of spatial patterns into other visual arrangements'. Frederiksen suggests that the reason why good visualizers do not recognize blurred pictures as early as do the poor visualizers is that they manipulate and transform the percept of a blurred picture to conform to whatever prior hypothesis is salient. Poor visualizers on the other hand, are less able to manipulate the clues provided by the stimulus picture and must alter their hypotheses instead. In conformity with this reasoning it was found that the poor visualizers made more guesses about the stimuli than did the good visualizers.

These findings of Frederiksen suggest that though visualizers may be able to produce more imaginative integrated responses to basically ambiguous stimuli, they are less efficient when it comes to producing correct solutions (recognition) to basically meaningful stimuli.

No answer has been given to the question with which this discussion began, though the leads suggested by the results of these studies are of sufficient interest to warrant further investigation. In the studies reported three different methods of measuring the visualizer-verbalizer continuum were employed. To what extent are they measuring the same thing? To what extent is it justified to treat the non-visualizer or poor visualizer as a verbalizer? Perhaps visualization is at one extreme but as one moves away from it the 'continuum' may branch into a verbalizer strand and a non-visualizer/non-verbalizer strand. To what extent does flexibility or controllability act as a moderator variable in studies of the kind reported here? These and many other questions must be asked before the relationship of an hypothesized visualizer-verbalizer variable to other cognitive style variables can be appreciated.

It should also be borne in mind that better predictions of performance on perceptual type tasks may be provided by some other cognitive variable such as category width (Tajfel, Richardson and Everstine, 1964) or field independence (Witkin and associates, 1954).

In concluding this section it is worth recalling one of the theoretical reasons why a visualizer-verbalizer dimension might be of importance. It has been argued by Sutcliffe (1962, 1963, 1964) that the greater likelihood of vivid imagers producing accurate reproductions of visually perceived patterns is due to their being 'literal' perceivers. This term has been used by other psychologists, e.g., Gibson and Gibson (1955) to refer to a perceptual style which emphasizes attention to the differences in sensory content that the objective world provides for us. The 'literal' perceiver is assumed to encode the stimulus in terms of its details while the 'schematic' perceiver (weak imagery; non-visualizer; verbalizer?) is assumed to encode stimuli by implicitly naming or classifying their salient features.

2. *What part does concrete imagery play in the activity of remembering and how does it relate to the more abstract or schematic memory based upon language?* This question is based upon the assumption, made already, that visual and linguistic modes of encoding, storing and decoding information are alternative strategies, though not mutually exclusive ones for most people. In the preceding question it was assumed that preferred strategies developed in different individuals and in extreme cases that these became habitual with little switching from one strategy to another. Overdependence upon one or other memory system each has its drawbacks, but some emphasis will be placed upon the need for a more detailed investigation of the processes associated with the concrete image memory because such a little is known about it. The problem of how an *abstract verbal memory* and a *concrete image memory* are related to one another will also be considered.

With the development of language ability during late childhood and adolescence more and more of our perceptual experiences are encoded in verbal terms. Early childhood experiences on the other hand are more likely to be encoded in terms of the sensory qualities of the environment. Part of the explanation for the almost total absence of memories for this early period may be due to this change in our principal means of encoding the information that arrives at our receptors. If this were so, then habitual visualizers should be able to recall more memories from the first seven years of life than habitual verbalizers. Why might this relation be expected?

First of all, the recovery of a past event requires the reinstatement of at least some part of the context within which the original event occurred. In a sensory conditioning study by Leuba (1940) for example, the ringing of a bell was several times paired with the actual smell of creosote. On a later occasion the sound of the bell alone resulted in a vivid olfactory image of creosote.

If experience were encoded in the form of sensory qualities during early childhood then it would be reasonable to expect that the recovery of many events from this period would require, either the occurrence of some unique physical stimulus associated with the original pattern of sensory qualities, or the arousal of some associated train of images. That children up to the age of about seven years are more likely to encode experience in terms of sensory qualities is suggested by the research of Kuhlman (1960). She hypothesized that at an early stage of language acquisition imagery may facilitate the covert rehearsal of name-object associations when the actual object is absent. Categories based on perceptual similarities or on temporal or spatial connections may also be formed on the basis of imagery. But when the more abstract categories of adult language are required dependence upon imagery is likely to impede development and so a change in cognitive mode is likely to take place.

To measure imagery differences Kuhlman used a combined index based upon four of the spatial tests found by Barratt (1953) to be associated with the spontaneous emergence of visual imagery. High and low scoring groups were matched for school grade (age), sex, and general intelligence. They were then compared on a task that required associating arbitrary verbal labels to pictures. High 'imagery' children performed significantly better at this task than low 'imagery' children and up to the age of six or seven a significant positive correlation was obtained between 'imagery' scores and results on conventional tests of school achievement, though beyond this age the correlation becomes insignificant. When high and low 'imagery' children were compared on a concept formation task, recognition of the attribute shared by a set of stimulus pictures was significantly slower among the high 'imagery' children. On the basis of her results Kuhlman concluded that children who retained a preference for utilizing visual imagery (habitual visualizers?) were inferior in their attainment of abstract concepts because they depended too much on the sensory qualities of the world.

Other evidence relating to the part played by imagery in the cognitive activities of children below the age of six or seven is suggested by the research of Reiff and Scheerer (1959). These investigators found that vivid and accurate childhood memories could be recovered under hypnosis; a procedure which encourages image thinking. Holt (1961) quotes several writers, mainly from the psychoanalytic schools, who are in agreement that: 'as one regresses from directed thought through reverie towards dreams, imagery (particularly the visual) becomes increasingly prominent and words much less so.' Finally it may be noted that some psycho-therapists (e.g., Reyher, 1963) encourage their patients to think in terms of images because this is believed to facilitate the recovery of childhood memories.

As we grow to adulthood in a modern industrialized society it is to be expected that verbal modes of encoding experience will take precedence over the imagery modes of early childhood. The structure of language imposes a more abstract form upon the way in which our experiences are stored and with the passage of time these experiences show the kind of conventionalization that Bartlett (1932) found in his serial reproduction experiments on memory. In a brilliant essay in which he contrasts what have been called here, the *abstract verbal memory* and the *concrete image memory*, Schachtel (1959) writes:

The processes of memory thus substitute the conventional cliché for the actual experience. It is true that the original experience or perception usually is already, to a large extent, determined by conventional cliché, by what the person expected to see or hear, which means by what he has been taught to expect. However, everybody who has paid attention to these processes in himself and others can observe that there is, especially at first, some awareness of the discrepancy between the experience itself and the thought or words which articulate, preserve, and express it. The experience is always fuller and richer than the articulate formula by which we try to be aware of it or to recover it. As time passes, this formula comes to replace more and more the original experience and, in addition, to become itself increasingly flat and conventionalized.

And again;

What is remembered is usually, more or less, only the fact that such an event took place. The signpost is remembered, not the place, the thing, the situation to which it points. And even these signposts themselves do not usually indicate the really significant moments in a person's life, rather they point to the events that are conventionally supposed to be significant, to the clichés which society has come to consider as the main stations of life. Thus the memories of the majority of people come to resemble increasingly the stereotyped answers to a questionnaire, in which life consists of time and place of birth, religious denomination, residence, educational degrees, job, marriage, number and birth dates of children, income, sickness and death.

The categories that the language of a society provides, and the amount of social reinforcement that is given for the utilization of these categories, are important factors influencing the degree of concreteness or abstractness of memories. Christopher Isherwood provides a wistful example in his novel *The World in the Evening*, of the 'loss of memory' which results when a switch is made from the concrete image memory of the child to the more abstract verbal memory of the adult.

I'd always remembered this window. It had a design of blue grapes and yellow leaves against a diamond of red. I must have spent hours at it, as a kid, peering out at the garden through the different colours of the glass; changing the scene, at will, from colour-mood to colour-mood and experiencing the pure pleasure of sensations which need no analysis . . . How had red felt, at the age of four? What had blue meant? Why was yellow? Perhaps, if I could somehow know that, now, I should understand everything else that had happened to me in the interval. But I never should know. The whole organ of cognition had changed, and I had nothing left to know with. If I looked through that window now, I should see nothing but a lot of adjectives.

It was noted earlier that a vivid image might be evoked if a unique stimulus from the original sensory context was presented. Most people have experienced the unexpected return of some long forgotten event or situation which persists briefly in a strongly imagined form. When the stimulus for such spontaneously imaged experiences is examined it is typically found to operate through a contact sense, like smell or touch, rather than a distance sense, like sight or hearing. To quote Schachtel once again:

The accidental recurrence of a bodily posture or of a sensory perception which he had experienced in the past, on some occasions brings with it the entire vision of that past, of the person he was then and of the way he saw things then. It is a sensation-feeling of a body posture or sensation of the perceptive apparatus—not a thought, as in willed recall, which revives the past. In Proust's account, visual sensations are far out-numbered as carriers of such memories by those of the lower more bodily senses such as the feeling of his own body in a particular posture, the touch of a napkin, the smell and taste of a flavour, the hearing of a sound—noise or melody, *not* the sound of words. All these sensations are far from conceptual thought, language, or conventional memory schemata. They renew a state of the psychosomatic entity, that in some respect, this entity had experienced before, felt before. It is as though they touched directly the unconscious memory trace, the record left behind by a total situation out of the past, whereas voluntary recall tries to approach and construct this past indirectly, coached and deflected by all these ideas, wishes and needs which tell the present person how the past could, should or might have been.

The essence of this distinction between what has been called a concrete image memory and an abstract verbal memory has its historical roots in the work of the French psychologists at the end of the last century, particularly Bergson (1911) and Ribot (1911).

From the evidence already cited by Reiff and Scheerer (1959) on hypnotic age regression, and from the work of Penfield and his associates (e.g., Penfield and Roberts, 1959) on the production of vivid memory images of specific events when the exposed temporal cortex of an epileptic patient is stimulated, it is clear that much of our past experience can be reconstructed or revived in a form very similar to that of the original experience itself. Whether it is *reconstructed*, or whether it is *revived*, is a crucial theoretical question in the field of human memory.

Interest in problems associated with human memory has grown enormously in the past ten years (e.g., Melton, 1963) but little attention has been devoted to the concrete memory image and its relation to more abstract memory schemata. How are the two related, if at all? The remainder of this section will be devoted to a discussion of some aspects of this question. It seems improbable that even the large storage capacity of the human brain could cope with each experiential chunk separately as well as storing a set of classifications and some kind of general index. In fact very little of the evidence concerning memorial processes accords with this library model. Even eidetic memories are seldom perfectly accurate though they may be detailed and vivid like the percepts on which they are based. Most memory theorists since the time of Bartlett (1932) have agreed that remembering any events that have been stored for more than a few minutes involves a process of *reconstruction* and not the *reviving* or 're-excitation of innumerable fixed, lifeless and fragmentary traces'. Whether some detail of a past event is recalled for reflective observation in the form of a 'picture' or in the form of sub-vocal description, it would be argued that it involves reconstruction. Even Proust's 'reliving' experiences, or those of Penfield's patients, do not prove 'the literalness with which past moments are permanently stored as discrete units' (Kubie, 1952).

Yet the notion that at least some sensory-affective experiences are stored in such a way that accurate total recall is possible is a notion that dies hard. When it occurs, as in some of the examples described by Reiff and Scheerer (1959) by what mechanism of reconstruction might it be achieved? Though this question ultimately requires a neuro-physiological answer there have been several attempts to provide a computor analogue. Such analogues provide a practical demonstration of the way in which discrete chunks of information can be encoded into sequences of binary numbers, combined with other similar chunks of information, and recoded into a shorter and therefore more economical sequences. When required the computor can be instructed to reconstruct and print out the original chunks of information (see Oldfield, 1954; Ross, 1961). At an introspective level a parallel to this process is found in the way in which we are aware of reconstructing a large amount of information from a mnemonic device or by means of some other rule or general principle. To lumber one's memory with masses of isolated dates concerning each day in each week for the past fifty years would be impossible, not to say ridiculous, but to remember a formula by which this information can be generated is relatively easy and enormously economical. In this instance however, no repacking of experience is involved. No one has ever acquired all this information in the form of discrete units, only the formula is learned. In some instances, of course, we do make use of numeric or linguistic devices for repacking new information after it has been acquired in a piecemeal fashion. But by what means do affective sensory experiences get repacked for economical storage? Numbers and words are connected together by their own internal logic. In the former this consists in the logical system of interrelated processes which are the foundation of mathematics, in the latter it is the logical system that makes up the grammar of a particular language. Once these basic numeric and linguistic 'programmes' have been learned, all kinds of storage economies can be introduced and optimal strategies of retrieval developed. Much sensory information regarding size, shape, position, colour and so on can be encoded in terms of numbers and names too, but how are they encoded so that a sensory-affective experience is revived which, at least, seems to be the same as the original? As we have seen already, words and numbers appear to carry information in an economical but skeletonized form. We retrieve the fact *that* I went sun bathing yesterday and *that* I saw Bill on the beach, but we do not typically retrieve in quasi sensory-affective form a re-experience of the sights, sounds, smells, tastes, pressures and temperatures that were involved in the original experience. Part of the difficulty is due to the social nature of numeric and linguistic symbol systems and the individual concrete nature of the images. Language and mathematics are social products that can be examined objectively. Though the codes provided by these two socially produced systems have a neuro-physiological substrate with its own code, it would seem that images and their interrelations provide nothing tangible to examine other *than* the code provided by their neuro-physiological substrate. Imagery does not provide a socially based set of lawfully related conventions and perhaps for this reason alone it is more difficult to study.

Because language is constrained by its grammatical structure some aspects of the associative process are predictable, but the relation of images to one another is organized idiosyncratically on the basis of emotional and motivational influences (Rapaport, 1951). The alternative to searching for some mechanism by which sensory affective experiences are *reconstructed* is to find some other mechanism which would enable them to be stored as whole units and simply *revived* or re-excited. Though Penfield's work has focused attention upon the temporal lobe as the only area of the cortex from which concrete memories of this kind can be produced, such evidence as we have comes entirely from epileptic patients. Would the same results be obtained from non-epileptic subjects? Quite apart from this problem is the more important one of interpreting the results. Because a past event in one's life is relived as a consequence of stimulating a unique point on the surface of the temporal lobe, no logical conclusions can be drawn regarding the neuro-physiological mechanism by which this conscious experience is produced. It is as reasonable to assume that a reconstruction mechanism has been activated as it is to assume that a unique set of concrete memories is stored in the minute cerebral structure that has been stimulated by the electrode.

3. *To what extent and in what ways do images supplement or modify our perceptual consciousness?* This question is concerned with the problem of enriched perception of a particular kind. An image by definition is a quasi-sensory or quasi-perceptual experience. Its meaning and significance derive from its differentiation from a percept. Though it has been stressed on several occasions that under certain conditions a subject may be unsure whether his phenomenal experience derives primarily from sensory or from non-sensory sources (i.e., is a percept or an image) it is only meaningful to talk of images when either the subject or the experimenter or preferably both have some adequate basis for making the assertion that an image is present in awareness. Criteria for the presence of an image must be as unequivocal as possible. In the context of imagery as discussed in this book it would be regarded as misleading to describe any response to an ink blot as due to the enrichment of the blot by images or even by imaginal processes unless specific evidence were available that this had occurred.

The fact that a well-integrated response of good form quality is produced to an ambiguous ink blot stimulus is not evidence that a process of enrichment is involved. We know that in learning to perceive and to recognize objects and events in the outside world (and the inside world) we build up categories and schemas that systematically bias our experience of the real world. A simple but dramatic example was suggested by the art historian E. H. Gombrich who noted the influence of national background upon the way in which we perceive the sounds made by a crowing cock. If we are English these sounds correspond approximately to the onamatapoeic phrase *cock-a-doodle-do*. If we are Dutch it is more likely to be heard as *ku-ke-le-ku* and if we are German the sounds are more 'accurately' represented by the phrase *ki-keri-ki*.

Apart from such long standing cognitive structures, perception is enriched by our transitory moods, expectations, needs and other motivational states. Energies from real world happenings are selected by our sensory apparatus and transformed into the electro-chemical energies of our neural circuits. They then interact with electro-chemical energies from non-sensory neural circuits concerned with memory and with the energies emanating from our internal sensory apparatus, to produce a particular response or pattern of responses. Under some circumstances these interacting neuro-physiological processes give rise to a conscious phenomenal experience. Such experiences present themselves typically as unified wholes. It seldom occurs that the contributory neuro-physiological activities have their concurrent counterparts at the phenomenal level.

These comments are very obvious but it is necessary to make them, so that no confusion shall arise in the use of the term *image* or in its relation to the notion of *enriched* perception.

Now consciousness of some aspect of the outside world may dawn gradually or it may simply present itself as immediately there. In this latter instance we most frequently employ the term *perception*. In the former the process is closer to that of *problem solving* in which we implicitly or explicitly set up hypotheses and check them. Often, though not always, a response to an ink blot is of this problem solving kind. We ask our subjects to tell us 'What might this be?' or 'What does this remind you of?'

It is at this point that imagery may in fact play some part in the production of the final response. Bartlett (1932) reports, for example, that one of his subjects . . .

. . . 'rummaged about' among his images to find one that would fit a given blot. He projected the image on to the blot. If he got a match, and there were still parts of the blot uncovered, he tried other images as nearly as possible related to the first.

Where no such process of conscious imaging is employed it adds nothing to our understanding of how the blot came to be enriched, to say that latent imagery must have been present. The significance of imagery can be only in our awareness of its presence and of what we are able to 'read' from it. It is a basic assumption that imagery is not merely an epiphenomenon but that our conscious awareness of its presence may make a difference to our behaviour. That being consciously aware of something has implications for behaviour, is an assertion that should be obvious but, like the study of imagery itself, it is only in the last decade that concern with the general issue of consciousness has been revived (see Collier, 1964; Maltzman, 1966).

The example provided by Bartlett's subject makes a clear distinction between the initial percept of the ink blot and the more meaningful images which were tried out in a search for a good fit. When the 'best' fit has been attained the blot is no longer perceived as a blot and the image is no longer present either. The phenomenal experience is an organized whole and the subject reports with varying degrees of satisfaction, and varying degrees of supporting detail, that he sees, for example, 'a huge fur covered bear'. What is more, it usually happens that the experimenter can see it too.

An extension of this process of relating images to percepts has been reported by some writers on eidetic ability. In the instances to be cited the phenomenal experience does not have the character of an organized whole, but the subject is usually aware that part of his visual world has been imaged and part has the quality of an ordinary perceptual experience.

Though such phenomena were discussed by the Marburg School of psychologists the first study to be mentioned here is one by Meenes (1933) who reported that some eidetic negro children were able to synthesize a figure consisting of a perceived part and an imaged part. A related kind of 'plastic perception' was found by Purdy (1936) in a normally adjusted female undergraduate. This girl had possessed eidetic imagery for as long as she could remember. For her . . .

. . . the world of actual perception is readily annihilated, as a whole or in part, and replaced by eidetic imagery. Thus, she can abolish the perception of a person who is standing before her open eyes, and in his place see an eidetic vision of some absent person . . . She can also add many kinds of eidetic details to the things in the real world, e.g., she can place green leaves upon barren winter trees, or supply a smooth shaven man with a full beard . . . (she) seldom mistakes her eidetic images for reality, but this does happen occasionally. Thus, when riding in an automobile, she has sometimes warned the driver against objects in the road which, as she soon discovered, were figments of her eidetic vision.

The possible relation of these phenomena to those of synaesthesia and the presence of undifferentiated inter-sensory boundaries is suggested by the effect of a vigorous but unexpected pull on this subject's outstretched arms while she was looking at a straight line 75 mm. long.

According to her report, the line appeared to expand by about 6 mm at either end, but, behaving like an elastic object, it returned to its normal length while the pull on her arms was still continuing.

Another, similar case to the one just described has been reported by the Russian psychologist Luria (1960). This subject was a young Moscow journalist named Shereshevskii who, among other unusual abilities, possessed an extraordinarily accurate memory. Synaesthesic percepts were very common in Shereshevskii's experience of the world. He also possessed eidetic imagery which sometimes resulted in a synthesis with his percepts and sometimes resulted in a complete suppression of some parts of his visual world. Luria writes:

Considerable difficulty in perception may be produced by the superimposition of the expected shape on the actual, by the discrepancy which occurs in each of us, but which actually passes unobserved and in any case does not disturb perception. Such a discrepancy in Shereshevskii sometimes played a vital role. 'It is enough that a man is not dressed in the suit I expect—and I expect it by the voice I hear when talking to him on the telephone—and I cannot recognize him, cannot agree that it is he . . . ' The discrepancy between the expected shape and the actual one more than once produced complete confusion in Shereshevskii's behaviour . . . 'I often noted' Shereshevskii related, 'that if I "see" a jug with milk on the left side of the table, and it's not there, I can't see it on the right-hand side—i.e., where it actually stands . . . and such things make me feel perplexed and stupid'.

Though these reports are in the nature of anecdotes the use of a binocular rivalry situation such as can be produced with the aid of a stereoscope might do much to unravel the subject and situational conditions under which some of these effects occur in eidetikers.

4. *How is the form and content of imagery influenced by motivational and emotional states?* This problem has been touched upon at several points earlier in this book and in discussing the concrete

image memory in this chapter. Interests have been seen to guide the form and content of an eidetic image and the presence of an unsolved problem during the hypnagogic state may motivate the emergence of a symbolic imagination image. Spontaneous memory images are likely to emerge into consciousness when an ongoing train of thought is blocked. The imagery at such times is not random but is relevant to the unsolved problem. In dream imagery and in the imagination imagery of an hallucination the content can often be traced to the prior motivational and emotional states of the dreamer or hallucinator.

The purpose of this orientating question is to emphasize that research is required, not only into the conditions that give rise to different classes of imagery, and not only into the relation of imagery to other cognitive processes, but also research is very much needed to show the reciprocal relation between imagery and motivational and emotional states.

One technique of investigating this latter problem is that of sensory conditioning. When some subjects have the expectation that a painful experience is going to occur but the actual stimulus fails to materialize, a pain may nevertheless be felt (Mowrer, 1960). The influence of expectation upon the emergence of an image has been demonstrated by Leuba and Dunlap (1951). An hypnotized subject . . .

. . . was shown a 3 x 5 in. white card on which a small diamond with the letter *S* in the center had been drawn with a red crayon. Simultaneously, a tin snapper was sounded for approximately 30 sec. Upon being awakened, amnesic for the hypnotic period, a brief conversation ensued after S was given a blank white card and asked to look at it and to report if anything should appear on it as he imagined various things: (1) eating and tasting roast beef, (2) smelling amonia, (3) hearing a metal snapper, (4) feeling velvet cloth, and (5) smoking a cigarette. S did not report anything on the card, except when imagining the sound of a snapper. At that point, he smiled, looked intently, and reported seeing a 'diamond'. E inquired: 'Any colour?' S replied: 'Yes, red; and there's a red S in the middle of the diamond'. S then turned the card over. 'It is there too. It's vague now and disappears'. After the design had disappeared, E actually snapped the snapper a number of times. S smiled, looked more intently at the card and said, 'It's there when you snap the snapper'. He examined the card carefully, and said 'What goes on here?'

In this hypnotic demonstration and in the normal waking incident described by Mowrer, the set or expectation was aroused by some associated cue. In both situations a quasi-sensory or quasi-perceptual experience resulted. The milk jug 'seen' at the wrong place on the table by Shereshevskii and the eidetic image of objects on a real road 'seen' by Purdy's subject may have their laboratory equivalents in these sensory conditioning studies. When better controlled investigations of sensory conditioning are undertaken in the future it might be expected that subjects with vivid imagery should condition more rapidly. Would highly introverted subjects (Eysenck, 1957) condition as quickly?

The phenomena itself is a remarkable one and of some theoretical interest. Why does not sensory conditioning always accompany motor conditioning? When a noxious stimulus is paired with a neutral one there is a combined sensory and motor response; for example we feel pain and remove our finger. When the neutral stimulus is presented by itself it usually elicits the motor element of what was previously a sensory-motor response. Why does not a conditioned sensory response always accompany the conditioned motor response? When both conditioned sensory and motor responses are evoked must the unconditioned stimulus have evoked some optimal degree of emotional arousal? Anecdotal evidence (Ribot, 1911) would certainly suggest that some degree of emotion is present during the acquisition of conditioned sensory-motor responses under everyday life conditions.

Concluding comments

Many aspects of imagery and imaging have been discussed, though not all in equal detail. Some aspects have been almost totally neglected, but enough has been said to indicate both the intrinsic interest and the significance of mental imagery for the study of cognitive functioning and cognitive development.

Between the innumerable questions that have been raised are a few facts, some hypotheses and many speculations. It is hoped that the next decade of psychological research will begin to reverse this pattern so that a more definitive account of mental imagery can be given.

Appendix A

THE BETTS QMI VIVIDNESS
OF IMAGERY SCALE*

Instructions for doing test

The aim of this test is to determine the vividness of your imagery. The items of the test will bring certain images to your mind. You are to rate the vividness of each image by reference to the accompanying rating scale, which is shown at the bottom of the page. For example, if your image is 'vague and dim' you give it a rating of 5. Record your answer in the brackets provided after each item. Just write the appropriate number after each item. Before you turn to the items on the next page, familiarize yourself with the different categories on the rating scale. Throughout the test, refer to the rating scale when judging the vividness of each image. A copy of the rating scale will be printed on each page. Please do not turn to the next page until you have completed the items on the page you are doing, and do not turn back to check on other items you have done. Complete each page before moving on to the next page. Try to do each item separately independent of how you may have done other items.

The image aroused by an item of this test may be:

Perfectly clear and as vivid as the actual experience	*Rating* 1
Very clear and comparable in vividness to the actual experience	*Rating* 2
Moderately clear and vivid	*Rating* 3
Not clear or vivid, but recognizable	*Rating* 4

* This scale was constructed as part of N.I.M.H. Project M-3950; J. P. Sutcliffe, Principal Investigator.

Vague and dim	*Rating* 5
So vague and dim as to be hardly discernible	*Rating* 6
No image present at all, you only 'knowing' that you are thinking of the object	*Rating* 7

An example of an item on the test would be one which asked you to consider an image which comes to your mind's eye of a red apple. If your visual image was moderately clear and vivid you would check the rating scale and mark '3' in the brackets as follows:

Item	*Rating*
5. A red apple	(3)

Now turn to the next page when you have understood these instructions and begin the test.

Think of some relative or friend whom you frequently see, considering carefully the picture that rises before your mind's eye. Classify the images suggested by each of the following questions as indicated by the degrees of clearness and vividness specified on the Rating Scale.

Item	*Rating*
1. The exact contour of face, head, shoulders and body	( )
2. Characteristic poses of head, attitudes of body, etc.	( )
3. The precise carriage, length of step, etc. in walking	( )
4. The different colours worn in some familiar costume	( )

Think of seeing the following, considering carefully the picture which comes before your mind's eye; and classify the image suggested by the following question as indicated by the degree of clearness and vividness specified on the Rating Scale.

5. The sun as it is sinking below the horizon	( )

Rating Scale

The image aroused by an item of this test may be:

Perfectly clear and as vivid as the actual experience	*Rating* 1
Very clear and comparable in vividness to the actual experience	*Rating* 2
Moderately clear and vivid	*Rating* 3

Not clear or vivid, but recognizable   *Rating* 4

Vague and dim   *Rating* 5

So vague and dim as to be hardly discernible   *Rating* 6

No image present at all, you only 'knowing' that you
    are thinking of the object   *Rating* 7

Think of each of the following sounds, considering carefully the image which comes to your mind's ear, and classify the images suggested by each of the following questions as indicated by the degrees of clearness and vividness specified on the Rating Scale.

Item	*Rating*
6. The whistle of a locomotive	( )
7. The honk of an automobile	( )
8. The mewing of a cat	( )
9. The sound of escaping steam	( )
10. The clapping of hands in applause	( )

Rating Scale

The image aroused by an item of this test may be:

Perfectly clear and as vivid as the actual experience   *Rating* 1

Very clear and comparable in vividness to the actual
    experience   *Rating* 2

Moderately clear and vivid   *Rating* 3

Not clear or vivid, but recognizable   *Rating* 4

Vague and dim   *Rating* 5

So vague and dim as to be hardly discernible   *Rating* 6

No image present at all, you only 'knowing' that you
    are thinking of the object   *Rating* 7

Think of 'feeling' or touching each of the following, considering carefully the image which comes to your mind's touch, and classify the images suggested by each of the following questions as indicated by the degrees of clearness and vividness specified on the Rating Scale.

Item	Rating
11. Sand	( )
12. Linen	( )
13. Fur	( )
14. The prick of a pin	( )
15. The warmth of a tepid bath	( )

Rating Scale

The image aroused by an item of this test may be:

Perfectly clear and as vivid as the actual experience	*Rating* 1
Very clear and comparable in vividness to the actual experience	*Rating* 2
Moderately clear and vivid	*Rating* 3
Not clear or vivid, but recognizable	*Rating* 4
Vague and dim	*Rating* 5
So vague and dim as to be hardly discernible	*Rating* 6
No image present at all, you only 'knowing' that you are thinking of the object	*Rating* 7

Think of performing each of the following acts, considering carefully the image which comes to your mind's arms, legs, lips, etc., and classify the images suggested as indicated by the degree of clearness and vividness specified on the Rating Scale.

Item	Rating
16. Running upstairs	( )
17. Springing across a gutter	( )
18. Drawing a circle on paper	( )
19. Reaching up to a high shelf	( )
20. Kicking something out of your way	( )

Rating Scale

The image aroused by an item of this test may be:

Perfectly clear and as vivid as the actual experience	*Rating* 1
Very clear and comparable in vividness to the actual experience	*Rating* 2
Moderately clear and vivid	*Rating* 3
Not clear or vivid, but recognizable	*Rating* 4
Vague and dim	*Rating* 5
So vague and dim as to be hardly discernible	*Rating* 6
No image present at all, you only 'knowing' that you are thinking of the object	*Rating* 7

Think of tasting each of the following considering carefully the image which comes to your mind's mouth, and classify the images suggested by each of the following questions as indicated by the degrees of clearness and vividness specified on the Rating Scale.

Item	*Rating*
21. Salt	( )
22. Granulated (white) sugar	( )
23. Oranges	( )
24. Jelly	( )
25. Your favourite soup	( )

Rating Scale

The image aroused by an item of this test may be:

Perfectly clear and as vivid as the actual experience	*Rating* 1
Very clear and comparable in vividness to the actual experience	*Rating* 2
Moderately clear and vivid	*Rating* 3
Not clear or vivid, but recognizable	*Rating* 4
Vague and dim	*Rating* 5
So vague and dim as to be hardly discernible	*Rating* 6
No image present at all, you only 'knowing' that you are thinking of the object	*Rating* 7

Think of smelling each of the following, considering carefully the image which comes to your mind's nose and classify the images suggested by each of the following questions as indicated by the degrees of clearness and vividness specified on the Rating Scale.

Item	Rating
26. An ill-ventilated room	( )
27. Cooking cabbage	( )
28. Roast beef	( )
29. Fresh paint	( )
30. New leather	( )

Rating Scale

The image aroused by an item of this test may be:

Perfectly clear and as vivid as the actual experience	*Rating* 1
Very clear and comparable in vividness to the actual experience	*Rating* 2
Moderately clear and vivid	*Rating* 3
Not clear or vivid, but recognizable	*Rating* 4
Vague and dim	*Rating* 5
So vague and dim as to be hardly discernible	*Rating* 6
No image present at all, you only 'knowing' that you are thinking of the object	*Rating* 7

Think of each of the following sensations, considering carefully the image which comes before your mind, and classify the images suggested as indicated by the degrees of clearness and vividness specified on the Rating Scale.

Item	Rating
31. Fatigue	( )
32. Hunger	( )
33. A sore throat	( )
34. Drowsiness	( )
35. Repletion as from a very full meal	( )

Rating Scale

The image aroused by an item of this test may be:

Perfectly clear and as vivid as the actual experience	*Rating*	1
Very clear and comparable in vividness to the actual experience	*Rating*	2
Moderately clear and vivid	*Rating*	3
Not clear or vivid, but recognizable	*Rating*	4
Vague and dim	*Rating*	5
So vague and dim as to be hardly discernible	*Rating*	6
No image present at all, you only 'knowing' that you are thinking of the object	*Rating*	7

Appendix B

THE GORDON TEST OF VISUAL
IMAGERY CONTROL*

You have just completed a questionnaire that was designed to measure the *vividness* of different kinds of imagery. In this present questionnaire some additional aspects of your imagery are being studie.

The questions are concerned with the ease with which you can *control* or *manipulate* visual images. For some people this task is relatively easy and for others relatively hard. One subject who could not manipulate his imagery easily gave this illustration. He visualized a table, one of whose legs suddenly began to collapse. He then tried to visualize another table with four solid legs, but found it impossible. The image of the first table with its collapsing leg persisted. Another subject reported that when he visualized a table the image was rather vague and dim. He could visualize it briefly but it was difficult to retain by any voluntary effort. In both these illustrations the subjects had difficulty in controlling or manipulating their visual imagery. It is perhaps important to emphasize that these experiences are in no way abnormal and are as often reported as the controllable type of image.

Read each question, then close your eyes while you try to visualize the scene described. Record your answer by underlining 'Yes', 'No' or 'Unsure', whichever is the most appropriate. Remember that your accurate and honest answer to these questions is most important for the validity of this study. If you have any doubts at all regarding the answer to a question, underline 'Unsure'. Please be certain that you answer each of the twelve questions.

---

* As it appears here the test is slightly altered from the form it had when first published by Gordon (1949).

APPENDIX B

1. Can you see a car standing in the road in front of a house?   Yes   No   Unsure

2. Can you see it in colour?   Yes   No   Unsure

3. Can you now see it in a different colour?   Yes   No   Unsure

4. Can you now see the same car lying upside down?   Yes   No   Unsure

5. Can you now see the same car back on its four wheels again?   Yes   No   Unsure

6. Can you see the car running along the road?   Yes   No   Unsure

7. Can you see it climb up a very steep hill?   Yes   No   Unsure

8. Can you see it climb over the top?   Yes   No   Unsure

9. Can you see it get out of control and crash through a house?   Yes   No   Unsure

10. Can you now see the same car running along the road with a handsome couple inside?   Yes   No   Unsure

11. Can you see the car cross a bridge and fall over the side into the stream below?   Yes   No   Unsure

12. Can you see the car all old and dismantled in a car-cemetery?   Yes   No   Unsure

156

REFERENCES

Allport, G. W., 'Eidetic Imagery', *Brit. J. Psychol.*, 1924, 15, 99–110
Allport, G. W., 'The Eidetic Image and the After Image', *Amer. J. Psychol.*, 1928, 40, 418–425.
Antrobus, J. S., Antrobus, J. S. & Singer, J. L., 'Eye Movements Accompanying Daydreaming, Visual Imagery and Thought Suppression', *J. Abnorm. Soc. Psychol.*, 1964, 69, 244–252
Ardis, J. A. & McKellar, P., Hypnagogic Imagery and Mescalin', *J. Ment. Sci.*, 1956, 102, 22–29
Armstrong, C. P., 'Some Notes on Imagery in Psychophysical Therapy', *J. Gen. Psychol.*, 1953, 48, 231–240
Arnold M. B., 'On the Mechanism of Suggestion and Hypnosis', *J. Abnorm. Soc. Psychol.*, 1946, 41, 107–128
As, A., A Factor Analytic Study of Some Subjective Personal Experiences and their Bearing on Theories of Hypnosis', *Acta Psychol.*, 1962, 20, 196–209
Bain, A., 'Mr. Galton's Statistics on Mental Imagery', *Mind*, 1880, 5, 564–573
Barber, T. A., 'Hypnotically Hallucinated Colours and their Negative After Images', *Amer. J. Psychol.*, 1964, 77, 313–318
Barratt, P. E., 'Imagery and Thinking', *Aust. J. Psychol.*, 1953, 5, 154–164
Barratt, P. E., 'Use of the EEG in the Study of Imagery', *Brit. J. Psychol.*, 1956, 47, 101–114
Barron, F., 'The Psychology of Imagination', *Sci. Amer.*, 1958, 199, 150–156
Barron, F., *Creativity and Psychological Health*, Van Nostrand, Princeton, 1963
Bartlett, F. C., *Remembering*, Cambridge Univ. Press, 1932
Bartlett, J. E. A., 'A Case of Organized Visual Hallucinations in an Old Man with Cataract, and their Relation to the Phenomena of the Phantom Limb', *Brain*, 1951, 74, 363–373
Bennet-Clark, H. C., & Evans, C. R., 'Fragmentation of Patterned Targets when Viewed as Prolonged After-images, *Nature*, 1963, 199, 1215–1216
Bentley, I. M., 'The Memory Image and its Qualitative Fidelity', *Amer. J. Psychol.*, 1899, 11, 1–48
Bergson, H., *Matter and Memory*. George Allen, 1911
Berry, W., 'The Fight of Colours in the After-image of a Bright Light', *Psychol. Bull.*, 1922, 19, 307–337
Berry, W., Colour Sequences in the After-image of White Light', *Amer J. Psychol.*, 1927, 38, 548–596
Berry, W. & Imus, H., Quantitative Aspects of the Flight of Colours. *Amer. J. Psychol.*, 1935, 47, 449–457
Betts, G. H., *The Distribution and Functions of Mental Imagery*, Teachers' College, Columbia University, 1909
Bexton, W. H., Heron, W. & Scott, T. H., 'Effects of Decreased Variation in the Sensory Environment, *Canad. J. Psychol.*, 1954, 8, 70–76

Bliss, E. L. & Clark, L. D., 'Visual Hallucinations', in L. J. West (Ed.) *Hallucinations*, Grune & Stratton, New York, 1962

Bond, I. K. & Hutchinson, H. C., 'Application of Reciprocal Inhibition Therapy to Exhibitionism', *Canad. Med. Ass. J.*, 1960, 83, 23–25

Boring, E. G., *Sensation and Perception in the History of Experimental Psychology*, Appleton-Century, New York, 1942

Bousfield, W. A. & Barry, H., 'The Visual Imagery of a Lightning Calculator', *Amer. J. Psychol.*, 1933, 45, 353–358

Brenman, M. & Gill, M. M., *Hypnotherapy: a Survey of the Literature*, Pushkin Press, London, 1947

Brindley, G. S., 'Two New Properties of Foveal After-images and a Photochemical Hypothesis to Explain Them', *J. Physiol.*, 1962, 164, 168–179

Brower, D., 'The Experimental Study of Imagery I. The Relation of Imagery to Intelligence, *J. Gen. Psychol.*, 1947, 31, 229–231

Brown, B. B., 'Specificity of EEG Photic Flicker Responses to Colour as Related to Visual Imagery Ability, *Psychophysiol.*, 1966, 2, 197–207

Brown, J. L., 'Afterimages', in C. H. Graham (Ed.) *Vision and visual perception*, Wiley, New York, 1965

Brownfield, C. A., *Isolation: Clinical and Experimental Approaches*, Alfred A. Knopf, New York, 1965

Bruner, J. S., Olver, R. R. & Greenfield, P. M., *Studies in Cognitive Growth*, Wiley, New York, 1966

Camberari, J. D., The Effect of Sensory Isolation on Suggestible and Nonsuggestible Psychology Graduate Students, unpublished doctoral dissertation, University of Utah, 1958. Cited in Freedman, S. J. & Marks, P. A., 'Visual Imagery Produced by Rhythmic Photic Stimulation', *Brit. J. Psychol.*, 1965, 56, 95–112

Carey, N., 'Factors in the Mental Processes of School Children I. Visual and Auditory Imagery, *Brit. J. Psychol.*, 1915, 7, 453–490

Chowdhury, K. R. & Vernon, P. E., 'An Experimental Study of Imagery and its Relation to Abilities and Interests, *Brit. J. Psychol.*, 1964, 55, 355–364

Clark, L. V., 'Effect of Mental Practice on the Development of a Certain Motor Skill', *Research Quarterly*, 1960, 31, 560–569

Cohen, L. D., Kipnis D., Kunkle, E. C. & Kubzansky, P. E., 'Observations of a Person with Congenital Insensitivity to Pain, *J. Abnorm. Soc. Psychol.*, 1955, 51, 333–338

Collier, R. M., 'Selected Implications from a Dynamic Regulatory Theory of Consciousness', *Amer. Psychol.*, 1964, 19, 265–269

Costa, A. M., 'L'effetto Geometrico-cromatico nella Stimolazione Intermittente della ochi Chiuse', *Arch. Psicol. Neurol. Psic.*, 1953, 14, 632–635

Costello, C. G., 'The Effects of Prefrontal Leucotomy upon Visual Imagery and the Ability to Perform Complex Operations', *J. Ment. Sci.*, 1956, 102, 507–516

Costello, C. G., 'The Control of Visual Imagery in Mental Disorder', *J. Ment. Sci.*, 1957, 103, 840–849

Costello, C. G. & McGregor, P., The Relationship Between Some Aspects of Visual Imagery and the Alpha Rhythm, *J. Ment. Sci.*, 1957, 103, 786–795

Coué, E., *Self Mastery through Conscious Autosuggestion*. Allen & Unwin, 1922

Craik, K. J. W., 'Origin of Visual After Images', *Nature*, 1940, 145, 512

Davis, F. C., 'The Functional Significance of Imagery Differences', *J. Exp. Psychol.*, 1932, 15, 630–661

Day, R. H., 'On Interocular Transfer and the Central Origin of Visual After-effects', *Amer. J. Psychol.*, 1958, 71, 784–790

Deckert, G. H., 'Pursuit Eye Movements in the Absence of a Moving Visual Stimulus', *Science*, 1964, 143, 1192–1193

Diehl, C. F., & England, N. C., 'Mental Imagery', *J. Speech Hear. Res.*, 1958, 1, 268–274

Doob, L. W., 'Eidetic Images among the Ibo', *Ethnology*, 1964, 3, 357–363

Doob, L. W., 'Exploring Eidetic Imagery among the Kamba of Central Kenya', *J. soc. Psychol.*, 1965, 67, 3–22

Doob, L. W., 'Eidetic Imagery: a Cross Cultural Will-o'-the-Wisp?', *J. Psychol.*, 1966, 63, 13–34

Downey, J., *The Creative Imagination*, Kegan Paul, 1929

Downie, J. E., 'An Experiment on Getting an After Image from a Mental Image', *Psychol. Rev.*, 1901, 8, 42–55

Drever, J., 'Some Observations on the Occipital Alpha Rhythm', *Quart. J. Exp. Psychol.*, 1955, 7, 91–97

Drever, J., 'Further Observations on the Relation Between EEG and Visual Imagery', *Amer. J. Psychol.*, 1958, 71, 270–276

Drewes, H. W., 'An Experimental Study of the Relationship Between Electroencephalographic Imagery Variables and Perceptual-Cognitive Processes', unpublished doctoral dissertation, Cornell University, 1958

El Koussy, A. A. H., 'An Investigation into the Factors in Tests Involving the Visual Perception of Space, *Brit. J. Psychol. Monogr. Suppl.*, 1935, No. 20

Ellis, H., *The World of Dreams*, Constable, New York, 1911

Eysenck, H. J., *The Structure of Human Personality*, Methuen, 1953

Eysenck, H. J., *The Dynamics of Anxiety and Hysteria*, Routledge & Kegan Paul, 1957

Fechner, G. T., (1860), *Elements of Psychophysics*, Holt, Rinehart & Winston, New York, 1966

Feinbloom, W., 'A Quantitative Study of the Visual After-image, *Arch, Psychol.*, 1938, 33, No. 233

Fernald, M. R., 'The Diagnosis of Mental Imagery', *Psychol. Rev. Monogr. Suppl.*, 1912, 14, No. 58

Fisher, S., 'Body Image Boundaries and Hallucinations', in L. J. West (Ed.) *Hallucinations*, Grune & Stratton, New York, 1962

Foulkes, D., Spear, P. S. & Symonds, J. D., 'Individual Differences in Mental Activity at Sleep Onset', *J. Abnorm. Psychol.*, 1966, 71, 280–286

Fox, C., 'The Conditions which Arouse Mental Images in Thought', *Brit. J. Psychol.*, 1914, 6, 420–431

Frederiksen, J. R., 'The Role of Cognitive Factors in the Recognition of Ambiguous Visual Stimuli', *ETS Research Bull.*, (RB–65–23). 1965

Freedman, S. J., Grunebaum, H. V., Stare, F. A. & Greenblatt, M., 'Imagery in Sensory Deprivation', in L. J. West (Ed.) *Hallucinations*, Grune & Stratton, New York, 1962

Freedman, S. J. & Marks, P. A., 'Visual Imagery Produced by Rhythmic Photic Stimulation: Personality Correlates and Phenomenology, *Brit. J. Psychol.*, 1965, 56, 95–112

Freides, D. & Hayden, S. P., 'Monocular Testing: a Methodological Note on Eidetic Imagery', *Percept. mot. Skills*, 1966, 23, 88

French, J. W., Ekstrom, R. B. & Price, L. A., *Manual for Kit of Reference Tests for Cognitive Factors* (Rev. 1963), Educational Testing Service, Princeton, New Jersey, 1963

Fromm, E., *The Forgotten Language*, Gollancz, 1952.

Furst, B., *The Practical Way to a Better Memory*, Fawcett World Library, New York, 1957

Galton, F., 'Statistics of Mental Imagery', *Mind*, 1880, 5, 300–318.

Galton, F. (1883), *Inquiries into Human Faculty*, Dent, 1905

Gastaut, H., 'The Brain Stem and Cerebral Electrogenesis in Relation to Consciousness', in J. F. Delafresnaye (Ed.) *Brain Mechanisms and Consciousness*, Blackwell, 1954

Gengerilli, J. A., 'Some Quantitative Experiments with Eidetic Imagery', *Amer. J. Psychol.*, 1930, 42, 399–404

Gerard, R. W., 'The Material Basis of Memory', *J. Verb. Learn. Verb. Behav.*, 1963, 2, 22–33

Gerard, R. W., 'Psychosynthesis: a Psychotherapy for the Whole Man', *Psychosynthesis Research Foundation*, Issue No. 14, Delaware, 1964

Ghiselin, B. (Ed.), *The Creative Process*. Univ. of California Press, Berkeley, 1952

Gibson, J. J. & Gibson, E. J., 'Perceptual Learning: Differentiation or Enrichment', *Psychol. Rev.*, 1955, 62, 32–41

Goldberger, L. & Holt, R. R., *'A Comparison of Isolation Effects and their Personality Correlates in Two Divergent Samples*, A.S.D. Tech. Rep. 61–417. Wright-Patterson A.F.B., Ohio, 1961

Goldstein, K. & Sheerer, M., 'Abstract and Concrete Behaviour: an Experimental Study with Special Tests', *Psychol. Monogr.*, 1941, 53, No.239

Goldstone, S., 'Psychophysics, Reality and Hallucinations', in L. J. West (Ed.) *Hallucinations*, Grune & Stratton, New York, 1962

Goldthwait, C., 'Relation of Eye Movements to Visual Imagery', *Amer. J. Psychol.*, 1933, 45, 106–110

Golla, F. L. & Antonovitch, S., 'The Relation of Muscular Tonus and the Patellar Reflex to Mental Work', *J. Ment. Sci.*, 1929, 75, 234–241

Golla, F. L., Hutton, E. L. & Walter, W. G., 'The Objective Study of Mental Imagery I. Physiological Concomitants', *J. Ment. Sci.*, 1943, 89, 216–223

Goodenough, D. R., Shapiro, A. Holden, M. & Steinschriber, L., 'A Comparison of "Dreamers" and "Nondreamers" ', *J. Abnorm. Soc. Psychol.*, 1959, 59, 295–302

Gordon, R., 'An Investigation into some of the Factors that Favour the Formation of Stereotyped Images', *Brit. J. Psychol.*, 1949, 39, 156–167

Gordon, R., 'An Experiment Correlating the Nature of Imagery with Performance on a Test of Reversal of Perspective, *Brit. J. Psychol.*, 1950, 41, 63–67

REFERENCES

Gregory, R. L., Wallace, J. G. & Campbell, F. W., 'Changes in the Size and Shape of Visual After-images Observed in Complete Darkness During Changes of Position in Space', *Quart, J. Exp, Psychol.*, 1959, 11, 54–56

Griffitts, C. H., *Fundamentals of Vocational Psychology*, Macmillan, New York, 1924

Griffitts, C. H., 'Individual Differences in Imagery', *Psychol. Monogr.*, 1927, 37, Whole No. 172

Haber, R. N. & Haber, R. B., 'Eidetic Imagery I: Frequency', *Percept. mot. Skills*, 1964, 19, 131–138

Hadamard, J., *An Essay on the Psychology of Invention in the Mathematical Field*, Dover, New York, 1954

Halpern, S., 'Hypno-introspection: a Contribution to the Theory of Hypnotherapy', Pt. 1. *J. Psychol.*, 1962, 53, 383–385

Halpern, S., Hypno-introspection: a Contribution to the Theory of Hypnotherapy', Pt. 2. *J. Psychol.*, 1964, 57, 329–376

Hanawalt, N. G., 'Recurrent Images: New Instances and a Summary of the Older Ones', *Amer. J. Psychol.*, 1954, 67, 170–174

Harano, K., Ogawa, K. & Naruse, G., 'A Study of Plethysmography and Skin Temperature During Active Concentration and Autogenic Exercise, in W. Luthe (Ed.) *Autogenic Training*, Grune & Stratton, New York, 1965

Harman, W. W., McKim, R. H., Mogar, R. E., Fadiman, J. & Stolaroff, M. J., 'Psychedelic Agents in Creative Problem Solving: a Pilot Study, *Psychol. Rep.*, 1966, 19, 211–227

Harris, C. S. & Haber, R. N., 'Selective Attention and Coding in Visual Perception', *J. Exp. Psychol.*, 1963, 65, 328–333

Hebb, D. O., 'The Problem of Consciousness and Introspection', in J. F. Delafresnaye (Ed.) *Brain Mechanisms and Consciousness*, Blackwell, 1954

Hicks, G. D., 'On the Nature of Images', *Brit. J. Psychol.*, 1924, 15, 121–148

Hill, D. S., 'An Experiment with an Automatic Mnemonic System', *Psychol. Bull.*, 1918, 15, 99–103

Höffding, H. (1891), *Outline of Psychology*, Macmillan, 1919

Holt, R. R., 'The Nature of T.A.T. Stories as Cognitive Products: a Psycho-analytic Approach', in J. Kagan & G. S. Lesser (Eds) *Contemporary Issues in Thematic Apperception Methods*, Charles C. Thomas, Springfield. 1961

Holt, R. R., 'Imagery: the Return of the Ostracized', *Amer. Psychol.*, 1964, 19, 254–264

Holt, R. R. & Goldberger, L., *Personological Correlates of Reactions to Perceptual Isolation*, WADC Tech. Rep. 59–753. Wright-Patterson A.F.B., Ohio, 1959

Homme, L. E., 'Perspectives in Psychology—XXIV: Control of Coverants, the Operants of the Mind, *Psychol. Rec.*, 1965, 15, 501–511

Horowitz, M. J., The Imagery of Visual Hallucinations,, *J. Nerv. Ment. Dis.*, 1964, 138, 513–523

Horowitz, M. J., 'Visual Imagery and Cognitive Organization', *Amer. J. Psychiat.*, 1967, 123, 938–946

Hovland, C. I. & Janis, I. L., *Personality and Persuasibility*. Yale Univ. Press, New Haven, 1959

Hume, D. (1748), *An Enquiry Concerning Human Understanding*, Open Court Publishing Co., Chicago, 1912

Humphrey, G., *Thinking: an Introduction to its Experimental Psychology*, Methuen, 1951

Hunter, I. M. L., 'Mnemonic Systems and Devices, *Science News*, 1956, 39, 75–97

Hyman, R. & Anderson, B., 'Solving Problems', *Inter. Sci. Technol.*, 1965, 45, 36–41

Isherwood, C., *The World in the Evening*, Methuen, 1954

Jackson, C. W. & Pollard, J. C., 'Sensory Deprivation and Suggestion: a Theoretical Approach', *Behav. Sci.*, 1962, 7, 332–342

Jackson, C. W. & Kelly, E. L., 'Influence of Suggestion and Subjects' Prior Knowledge in Research on Sensory Deprivation', *Science*, 1962, 135, 211–212

Jacobson, E., 'Electrophysiology of Mental Activities', *Amer. J. Psychol.*, 1932, 44, 677–694

Jaensch, E. R., *Eidetic Imagery*, Kegan Paul, 1930

James, W., *Essays in Radical Empiricism*, Longmans, Green, 1912

Jasper, H. H. & Cruickshank, R. M., 'Electro-encephalography II. Visual Stimulation and the After-image as Affecting the Occipital Alpha Rhythm, *J. Gen. Psychol.*, 1937, 17, 29–48

Jenkin, A. M., 'Imagery and Learning', *Brit. J. Psychol.*, 1935, 26, 149–164

Juhasz, J. B. & Sarbin, T. R., 'Imagination, Imitation and Role Taking', a paper read to the American Psychological Association, Washington D.C., August, 1967

Kahn, T. C., 'Theoretical Foundations of Audio-visual-tactile Rhythmic Induction Experiments', *Science*, 1954, 120, 103–104

Kamiya, J. & Zeitlin, D., 'Learned EEG Alpha Wave Control by Humans', *Report No. 183, Department of Mental Hygiene, Research Division*, Calif., 1963

Kanner, L., *Child Psychiatry* (3rd Ed.). Charles C. Thomas, Springfield, 1957

Kellogg, R., Knoll, M. & Kugler, J., 'Form Similarity between Phosphenes of Adults and Pre-school Children's Scribbling', *Nature*, 1965, 208, 1129–1130

Kerr, M. & Pear, T. H., 'Unseen Drama and Imagery: some Experimental Observations', *Brit. J. Psychol.*, 1931, 22, 43–54

Kline, M. V., 'Visual Imagery and a Case of Experimental Hypnotherapy', *J. Gen. Psychol.*, 1952, 46, 159–167

Klüver, H., 'An Experimental Study of the Eidetic Type', *Genet. Psychol. Monogr.*, 1926, 1, 70–230

Klüver, H., 'Mescal Visions and Eidetic Vision', *Amer. J. Psychol.*, 1926a, 37, 502–515

Klüver, H., 'Studies on the Eidetic Type and on Eidetic Imagery', *Psychol. Bull.*, 1928, 25, 69–104

Klüver, H., *Mescal: the 'Divine' Plant and its Psychological Effects*, Kegan Paul, 1928a

Klüver, H., 'Fragmentary Eidetic Imagery', *Psychol. Rev.*, 1930, 37, 441–458

Klüver, H., 'The Eidetic Child', in C. Murchison (Ed.) *A Handbook of Child Psychology*, Clark Univ. Press, Worcester, 1931

Klüver, H., 'Eidetic Phenomena', *Psychol. Bull.*, 1932, 29, 181–203

Klüver, H., 'Mechanisms of Hallucinations', in Q. McNemar & M. A. Merrill (Eds) *Studies in Personality: Contributed in Honour of Lewis M. Terman*, McGraw-Hill, New York, 1942

Knoll, M. Kugler, J., Eichmeier, J. & Höfer, O., 'Note on the Spectroscopy of Subjective Light Patterns', *J. Analyt. Psychol.*, 1962, 7, 55–69

Knoll, M. & Kugler, J., 'Subjective Light Pattern Spectroscopy in the Electroencephalographic Range', *Nature*, 1959, 184, 1823

Knoll, M. & Kugler, J., 'Pulse Current Analysis of Elementary Visual Hallucinations by Coincidence Circuits in the Brain', *Inter. Conf. Micro waves, Circuit Theory, Information Theory*, Pt. 2, Tokyo, Japan, 1964

Krutetski, V. A., 'Some Characteristics of the Thinking of Pupils with Little Capacity for Mathematics', in Simon, B. & Simon, J. (Eds) *Educational Psychology in the U.S.S.R.*, Routledge, 1963

Kubie, L. S., 'Discussion on Papers by Drs. Cobb and Penfield', *A.M.A Arch. Neurol. Psychiatr.*, 1952, 67, 191–195

Kubzansky, P. E., 'Creativity, Imagery and Sensory Deprivation', *Acta Psychol.*, 1961, 19, 507–508

Kuhlman, C., Visual Imagery in Children', unpublished doctoral dissertation, Harvard University, 1960 (mimeographed summary). Some results of this study are presented and discussed in Bruner, J. S. *et al. Studies in cognitive growth*. Wiley, New York, 1966

Külpe, O. (1893), *Outlines of Psychology*, Swan Sonnenschein, London (3rd Ed.) 1909

Ladd, G. T., 'Contribution to the Psychology of Visual Dreams', *Mind* (N.S.), 1892, 1, 299–304

Langfeld, H. S., 'Note on a Case of Chromaesthesia', *Psychol. Bull.*, 1914, 11, 113–114

Lay, W., 'Mental Imagery', *Psychol. Rev. Monogr. Suppl.*, 1897, 92, 1–59

Lazarus, A. A., 'The Treatment of Chronic Frigidity by Systematic Desensitization', *J. Nerv. Ment. Dis.*, 1963, 136, 272–278

Lazarus, A. A., 'Crucial Procedural Factors in Desensitization Therapy, *Behav. Res. Ther.*, 1964, 2, 65–70

Leaning, F. E., 'An Introductory Study of Hypnagogic Phenomena', *Proc. Soc. Psychic, Res.*, 1926, 35, 289–409

Leiderman, P. H., 'Imagery and Sensory Deprivation', *Proc. Third World Congress Psychiatr.*, 1964, 227–231

Leon, H. V. & Arnhoff, F. N., 'Cognitive and Perceptual Disturbances in Short Term Sensory Deprivation as a Function of Differential Expectancy Levels', *J. gen. Psychol.*, 1965, 73, 169–176

Leuba, C., 'Images as Conditioned Sensations', *J. Exp. Psychol.*, 1940, 26, 345–351

Leuba, C. & Dunlap, R., 'Conditioning Imagery', *J. Exp. Psychol.*, 1951, 41, 352–355

Leuner, H., 'The Interpretation of Visual Hallucinations', in *Psychopathology and Pictorial Expression*, Sandoz, 1963

Lewin, K. 'Behaviour and Development as a Function of the Total Situation', in L. Carmichael (Ed.). *Manual of child psychology*, Wiley, New York, 1946

Luria, A. R., 'Memory and the Structure of Mental Processes, *Problems of Psychology*, 1960, 1 & 2, 81–93

Luria, A. R., 'Neuropsychological Analysis of Focal Brain Lesions', in B. J. Wolman (Ed.), *Handbook of Clinical Psychology*, McGraw-Hill, New York, 1965

MacIndoe, I. & Singer, G., 'Imaging in Spontaneous Hallucinators', *Psychol. Rec.*, 1966, 16, 81–86

McBain, W. N., 'Imagery and Suggestibility: a Test of the Arnold Hypothesis', *J. Abnorm. Soc. Psychol.*, 1954, 49, 36–44

McGuigan, F. J., 'Covert Oral Behaviour and Auditory Hallucinations', *Psycho physiol.*, 1966, 3, 73–80

McKellar, P., *Imagination and Thinking*, Cohen & West, 1957

McKellar, P., 'Three Aspects of the Psychology of Originality in Human Thinking', *Brit. J. Aes.*, 1963, 3, 129–147

McKellar, P., 'Differences of Mental Imagery', *The Mensa Correspondence* 1963a, 51, 1–5

McKellar, P., 'Thinking, Remembering and Imagining', in J. G. Howells (Ed.), *Modern Perspectives in Child Psychiatry*, Oliver & Boyd, Edinburgh, 1965

McKellar, P. & Simpson, L., 'Between Wakefulness and Sleep: Hypnagogic Imagery', *Brit. J. Psychol.*, 1954, 45, 266–276

Maltzman, I., 'Awareness: Cognitive Psychology vs. Behaviourism, *J. Exp. Res. Person.*, 1966, 1, 161–165

Maury, L. F. A., *Le Sommeil et les Rêves*, Paris, 1861 (not seen)

Meenes, M., 'Eidetic Phenomena in Negro School Children', *Psychol. Bull.*, 1933, 30, 688–689

Meenes, M. & Morton, M. A., 'Characteristics of the Eidetic Phenomenon', *J. Gen. Psychol.*, 1936, 14, 370–391

Melton, A. W. (Ed.), 'Meetings on Memory. A.A.A.S. Philadelphia 1962', *J. Verb. Learn. Verb. Behav.*, 1963, 2, Whole Issue

Michael, W. B., 'The Nature of Space and Visualization Abilities: some Recent Findings Based on Factor Analysis Studies', *Trans. New York Acad. Sci.*, Series 2, 1949, 11, 275–281

Moore, D. W. & Ross, J., 'A Fast Principal Components Factor Analysis Program for the IBM 1620', *Ed. Psychol. Meas.*, 1964, 24, 675–676

Morgan, R. F. & Bakan, P., 'Sensory Deprivation Hallucinations and other Sleep Behaviour as a Function of Position, Method of Report, and Anxiety', *Percept. mot. Skills*, 1965, 20, 19–25

Morsh, J. E. & Abbott, H. D., 'An Investigation of After-images', *J. Comp. Pyschol.*, 1945, 38, 47–63

Mowrer, O. H., *Learning Theory and the Symbolic Process*, Wiley, New York, 1960

Munday-Castle, A. C., 'Electrophysiological Correlates of Intelligence', *J. Person.*, 1958, 26, 184–199

Myers, T. I. & Murphy, D. B., 'Reported Visual Sensations during Brief Exposure to Reduced Sensory Input', in L. J. West (Ed.) *Hallucinations*. Grune & Stratton, New York, 1962

Myers, F. W. H., *Human Personality and its Survival of Bodily Death*, Longmans, Green & Co. 1903

REFERENCES

Myklebust, H. R., *The Psychology of Deafness* (2nd Ed.), Grune & Stratton, New York, 1964

Ogden, R. M., 'Experimental Criteria for Differentiating Memory and Imagination in Projected Visual Images', *Psychol. Rev.*, 1913, 30, 378–410

Ohwaki, Y. & Kihara, T., 'A New Research on the So-called "Bocci" Image', *Tohoku Psychologica Folia*, 1953, 13, 157–180

Oldfield, R. C., 'Memory Mechanisms and the Theory of Schemata', *Brit. J. Psychol.*, 1954, 45, 14–23

Orne, M. T., 'On the Social Psychology of the Psychological Experiment', *Amer. Psychol.*, 1962, 17, 776–783

Osgood, C. E., Suci, J. & Tannenbaum, P. H., *The Measurement of Meaning*, University of Illinois, Urbana, 1957

Oster, G., 'Phosphenes,' *Art. Inter.*, 1966, 10, 43–46

Oswald, I., 'After-images from Retina and Brain', *Quart. J. Exp. Psychol.*, 1957, 9, 88–100

Oswald, I., 'The EEG Visual Imagery and Attention', *Quart. J. Exp. Psychol.*, 1957a, 9, 113–118

Oswald, I., 'A Case of Fluctuation of Awareness with the Pulse', *Quart. J. Exp. Psychol.*, 1959, 11, 45–48

Oswald, I., *Sleeping and Waking*, Elsevier Publishing Co., Amsterdam, 1962

Paivio, A., 'Learning of Adjective-noun Paired-associates as a Function of Adjective-noun Word Order and Noun Abstractness', *Canad. J. Psychol.*, 1963, 17, 370–379

Paivio, A., 'Abstractness, Imagery, and Meaningfulness in Paired-associate Learning', *J. Verb. Learn. Verb. Behav.*, 1965, 4, 32–38

Partridge, G. E., 'Reveries', *Ped. Sem.*, 1898, 5, 445–474

Paterson, A. S., 'The Respiratory Rhythms in Normal and Psychotic Subjects', *J. Neurol. Psychopath.*, 1935, 16, 36–53

Pear, T. H., 'Recent Investigations on Visual Imagery with Special Reference to Hallucinations', *J. Ment. Sci.*, 1927, 73, 195–199

Pear, T. H., 'Mental Imagery and Style in Writing', *University of Toronto Quart.*, 1935, 4, 453–467

Pear, T. H., 'The Place of Imagery in Mental Processes', *Bull. John Rylands Lib.*, 1937, 21, 193–214

Peck, L. & Hodges, A. B., 'A Study of Racial Differences in Eidetic Imagery of Preschool Children', *J. Genet. Psychol.*, 1937, 51, 141–161

Peck, L. & Walling, R., 'A Preliminary Study of the Eidetic Imagery of Preschool Children', *J. Genet. Psychol.*, 1935, 47, 168–192

Penfield, W., 'Memory Mechanisms', *A.M.A. Arch. Neurol. Psychiatr.*, 1952, 67, 178–191

Penfield, W. & Roberts, L., *Speech and Brain Mechanisms*, Princeton Univ. Press, Princeton, 1959

Perky, C. W., 'An Experimental Study of Imagination', *Amer. J. Psychol.*, 1910, 21, 422–452

Perot, P. & Penfield, W., 'Hallucinations of Past Experience and Experiential Responses to Stimulation of Temporal Cortex', *Amer. Neural. Ass. N.Y. Trans.*, 1960, 85, 80–84

Pinard, W. J., 'Spontaneous Imagery: its Nature, Therapeutic Value, and

Effect on Personality Structure', *Boston University Graduate Journal*, 1957, 5, 150–153

Popov, N. A. & Popov, C., 'Contribution à l'étude des fonctions corticales chez l'homme, par la méthode des réflexes conditionnés electrocorticaux. I. Action de l'alcool sur les images consecutives, et leur conditionnement', *C.R. Acad. Sci.*, 1953, 237, 930–932

Popov, N. A. & Popov, C., 'Contribution à l'étude des fonctions corticales chez l'homme par la méthode des réflexes conditionnés electrocorticaux. V. Deuxième système de signalisation', *C.R. Acad. Sci.* 1954, 238, 2118–2120

Prentiss, D. W. & Morgan, F. P., 'Anhalonium (Mescal button)'. *Therap. Gaz.* (3rd Series), 1895, 19, 577 (not seen)

Pritchard, R. M., Heron W. & Hebb, D. O., 'Visual Perception approached by the Method of Stabilized Images', *Canad. J Psychol.*, 1960, 14, 67–77

Purdy, D. M., 'Eidetic Imagery and Plasticity of Perception', *J. Gen. Psychol.*, 1936, 15, 437–453

Ranken, H. B., 'Language and Thinking; Positive and Negative Effects of Naming', *Science*, 1963, 141, 48–50

Ranken, H. B., 'Use of Names in Concept Formation', *Science*, 1963a, 141, 1238–1240

Rapaport, D., *'Organization and Pathology of Thought'*, Columbia Univ. Press, New York, 1951

Reiff, K. & Sheerer, M., *Memory and Hypnotic Age Regression'*, International Universities Press, New York, 1959

Reinhold, D. B., 'Effect of Training on Perception of After-images', *Percept. mot. Skills*, 1957, 7, 198

Reyher, J., 'Free Imagery: an Uncovering Procedure', *J, Clin. Psychol.*, 1963, 19, 454–459

Ribot, T. A., *The Psychology of Emotion* (2nd Ed.) London: Scott, 1911

Richardson, A., unpublished data on personality correlates of imaging abilities, 1962

Richardson, A., 'The Place of Subjective Experience in Contemporary Psychology', *Brit. J. Psychol.*, 1965, 56, 223–232

Richardson, A., 'Imagery and Meaning', a paper read to the 21st Annual Conference, British Psychological Society (Australian Branch), Sydney, August, 1965a

Richardson, A., 'Mental Practice: a Review and Discussion,' (1). *Research Quarterly*, 1967a, 38, 95–107

Richardson, A., 'Mental Practice: a Review and Discussion,' (2). *Research Quarterly*, 1967b, 38, 263–273

Richardson, A. & Start, K. B., 'Imagery and Mental Practice', *Proceed. XVII Internat. Congress Psychol., Washington, 1963*, North Holland Publishing Co., Amsterdam, 1964.

Rimland, B. *Infantile Autism: the Syndrome and its Implications for a Neural Theory of Behaviour*, Appleton-Century-Crofts, New York, 1964

Robbins, S. & Robbins, R., *Speech Sound Discrimination Tests*, Expression Co., Boston, 1948

Roe, A., 'A Study of Imagery in Research Scientists', *J. Person.*, 1951, 19, 459–470

REFERENCES

Rosenblith, W. A., Miller, G. A., Egan, J. P., Hirsh, I. J., & Thomas, G. J., 'An Auditory After-image?', *Science*, 1947, 106, 333–334

Ross, J., 'Human Memory: a Partial Model and its Implications for Retroactive Phenomena', Tech. Rep., Psychology Dept., Princeton University, 1961

Ross, J., and Lawrence, K. A., 'Some Observations on Memory Artifice, *Psychon. Sci.*, 1968, 13, 107–108

Rossi, A. M., Sturrock, J. B. & Solomon, P., 'Suggestion Effects on Reported Imagery in Sensory Deprivation', *Percept. mot. Skills*, 1963, 16, 39–45

Rowan, H. (Ed.), 'Thinking About Thinking with Brain and Computer', *Carnegie Corp. New York Quart.*, 1965, 13, 41–42

Russell, B., *An Outline of Philosophy*, Allen & Unwin, 1927

Schachtel, E. G., *Metamorphosis*, Basic Books, New York, 1959

Schaub, A. de Vries, 'On the Intensity of Images', *Amer. J. Psychol.*, 1911, 22, 346–368

Scheibel, M. E. & Scheibel, A. B., 'Hallucinations and the Brain Stem Reticular Core', in L. J. West (Ed.), *Hallucinations*, Grune & Stratton, New York, 1962

Schlagel, T. F., 'The Dominant Method of Imagery in Blind as Compared to Sighted Adolescents', *J. Genet. Psychol.*, 1953, 83, 265–277

Schmeidler, G. R., Visual Imagery Correlated to a Measure of Creativity', *J. Consult. Psych.*, 1965, 29, 78–80

Segal, S. J., personal communication, 1964

Segal, S. J. & Nathan, S., 'The Perky Effect: Incorporation of an External Stimulus into an Imagery Experience under Placebo and Control Conditions', *Percept. Mot. Skills*, 1964, 18, 385–395

Seitz, P. E. D. & Molholm, H. B., 'Relation of Mental Imagery to Hallucinations', *A.M.A. Arch. Neurol. Psychiat.*, 1947, 57, 469–480

Sheehan, P. W., 'Accuracy and Vividness of Visual Images', *Percept. mot. Skills*, 1966a, 23, 391–398

Sheehan, P. W., 'Functional Similarity of Imaging to Perceuving: Individual Differences in Vividness of Imagery', *Percept. mot. Skills*, 1966b, 23, 1011–1033

Sheehan, P. W., 'A Shortened Form of Betts' Questionnaire upon Mental Imagery', *J. Clin. Psychol.*, 1967a, 23, 386–389

Sheeham, P. W., 'Reliability of a Short Test of Imagery', *Percept. mot. Skills*, 1967b, 25, 744

Sheehan, P. W., 'Visual Imagery and the Organizational Properties of Perceived Stimuli', *Brit. J. Psychol.*, 1967c, 58, 247–252

Sheehan, P. W., 'Colour Response to the TAT: an Instance of Eidetic Imagery?', *J. Psychol.*, 1968, 68, 203–209

Shipton, J. & Walter, W. Grey, 'Les relations entre les activités alpha, les modes de pensée et les affinités sociales', *EEG Clin. Neurophysiol.*, 1957, Suppl. No. 6, 185–202

Short, P. L., 'The Objective Study of Mental Imagery', *Brit. J. Psychol.*, 1953, 44, 38–51

Short, P. L. & Walter, W. G., 'The Relationship Between Physiological Variables and Stereognosis', *EEG Clin. Neurophysiol.*, 1954, 6, 29–44

Short, R. R. & Oskamp, S., 'Lack of Suggestion Effects on Perceptual

Isolation (sensory deprivation) Phenomena', *J. Nerv. Ment. Dis.*, 1965, 141, 190–194

Shurley, J. T., 'Hallucinations in Sensory Deprivation and Sleep Deprivation', in L. J. West (Ed.) *Hallucinations*, Grune & Stratton, New York, 1962

Siipola, E. M. & Hayden, S. D., 'Exploring Eidetic Imagery among the Retarded', *Percept. mot. Skills*, 1965, 21, 275–286

Silberer, H. (1909), 'Report on a Method of Eliciting and Observing Certain Symbolic Hallucination Phenomena', in D. Rapaport (Ed.), *Organization and Pathology of Thought*, Columbia Univ. Press, New York, 1951

Silverman, A. J., Cohen, S. I., Shmavonian, B. M. & Greenberg, G., 'Psychophysiological Investigations in Sensory Deprivation', *Psychosom. Med.*, 1961, 23, 48–61

Simpson, H. M., Paivio, A. & Rogers, T. B., 'Occipital Alpha Activity of High and Low Visual Imagers During Problem Solving', *Psychon. Sci.*, 1967, 8, 49–50

Simpson, L. & McKellar, P., 'Types of Synaesthesia', *J. Ment. Sci.*, 1955, 100, 143–147

Singer, J. L., 'Imagination and Waiting Ability in Young Children', *J. Person.*, 1961, 29, 396–413

Singer, J. L. & Antrobus, J. S., 'A Factor-analytic Study of Daydreaming and Conceptually-related Cognitive and Personality Variables', *Percept. mot. Skills*, Monogr. Supple. 1963

Singer, J. L. & Antrobus, J. S., 'Eye Movements During Fantasies', *Arch. gen. Psychiatr.*, 1965, 12, 71–76

Slatter, K. H., 'Alpha Rhythm and Mental Imagery', *EEG Clin. Neurophysiol.*, 1960, 12, 851–859

Smith, I. McFarlane, *Spatial Ability*, Univ. of London Press, 1964

Smith, R. K. & Noble, C. E., 'Effects of a Mnemonic Technique Applied to Verbal Learning and Memory', *Percept. mot. Skills*, 1965, 21, 123–134

Smythies, J. R., 'The Stroboscopic Patterns (II): The Phenomenology of the Bright Phase and After-images', *Brit. J. Psychol.*, 1959, 50, 305–324

Smythies, J. R., 'The Stroboscopic Patterns (III): Further Experiments and Discussion', *Brit. J. Psychol.*, 1960, 51, 247–255

Solomon, P. & Mendelson, J., 'Hallucinations in Sensory Deprivation', in L. J. West (Ed.). *Hallucinations*, Grune & Stratton, New York, 1962

Sperling, G., 'The Information Available in Brief Visual Presentations', *Psychol. Monogr. Gen. Appl.*, 1960, 74, No. 11

Sperling, G., Negative After-image Without Prior Positive Image', *Science*, 1960a, 131, 1613–1614

Sperling, G., 'A Model for Visual Memory Tasks', *Human Factors*, 1963, 5, 19–31

Stark, S., 'Role-taking, Empathic Imagination, and Rorschach Human Movement Responses: a Review of Two Literatures', *Percept. mot. Skills*, 1966, 23, 243–256

Start, K. B. & Richardson, A., 'Imagery and Mental Practice', *Brit. J. Ed. Psychol.*, 1964, 34, 280–284

Stewart, C. A. & Smith, I. MacFarlane, 'The Alpha Rhythm, Imagery and Spatial and Verbal Abilities', *Durham Res. Rev.*, 1959, 2, 272–286

REFERENCES

Stout, G. F. (1898), *A Manual of Psychology* (2nd Ed.), University Tutorial Press, London, 1907

Sullivan, H. S., *Conceptions of Modern Psychiatry*, William Allanson White Psychiatric Foundation, Washington, D.C., 1947

Sully, J., *The Human Mind: a Textbook of Psychology*. Longmans Green, 1892

Sully, J., *Illusions: a Psychological Study* (4th Ed.), Kegan Paul, 1905

Sumner, F. C. & Watts, F. P., 'Rivalry between Uniocular Negative After-images and the Vision of the Other Eye', *Amer. J. Psychol.*, 1936, 48, 109–116

Sutcliffe, J. P., 'The Relation of Imagery and Fantasy to Hypnosis', progress report on N.I.M.H., Project M–3950, University of Sydney, Australia, 1962

Sutcliffe, J. P., 'The Relation of Imagery and Fantasy to Hypnosis', progress report on N.I.M.H., Project M–3950, University of Sydney, Australia, 1963

Sutcliffe, J. P., 'The Relation of Imagery and Fantasy to Hypnosis', progress report on N.I.M.H., Project M–3950, University of Sydney, Australia, 1964

Sutcliffe, J. P., 'The Relation of Imagery and Fantasy to Hypnosis', final report on N.I.M.H., Project M–3950, University of Sydney, Australia, 1965

Swindle, P. F., 'Positive After-images of Long Duration', *Amer. J. Psychol.*, 1916, 27, 324–334

Swindle, P. F., 'Visual, Cutaneous and Kinaesthetic Ghosts', *Amer. J. Psychol.*, 1917, 28, 349–372

Tajfel, H., Richardson, A. & Everstine, L., 'Individual Differences in Categorizing: a Study of Judgmental Behaviour', *J. Person.*, 1964, 32, 90–108

Tauber, E. S. & Green, M. R., *Prelogical Experience*, Basic Books, New York, 1959

Taylor, J. M., 'A Comparison of Delusional and Hallucinatory Individuals Using Field Dependency as a Measure', unpublished doctoral dissertation, Purdue University, 1956; cited by Witkin, H. A., Dyk, R. B., Faterson, H. F., Goodenough, D. R. & Karp, S. A. *Psychological Differentiation: Studies of Development*, Wiley, New York, 1962

Teasdale, H. H., 'A Quantitative Study of Eidetic Imagery', *Brit. J. Ed. Psychol.*, 1934, 4, 56–74

Thale, T., Westcott, G. & Salomon, K., 'Hallucinations and Imagery Induced by Mesalin', *Amer. J. Psychiat.*, 1950, 106, 686–691

Thurstone L. L., 'Factor Analysis', in M. H. Marx (Ed.), *Psychological Theory*, MacMillan, New York, 1951

Traxel, W. Kritische untersuchungen zur eidetik, *Archiv. für die gesamte Psychologie*, 1962, 114, 260–336

Tyrrell, G. N. M., *Apparitions*, Duckworth, 1953

Vernon, J. A., *Inside the Black Room*, Clarkson N. Potter Inc., 1963

Walkup, L. E., 'Creativity in Science Through Visualization', *Percept. mot. Skills*, 1965, 21, 35–41

Wallis, G., *The Art of Thought*, Harcourt, New York, 1926

Walter, R. D. & Yeager, C. L., 'Visual Imagery and Electroencephalographic Changes', *EEG Clin. Neurophysiol.*, 1956, 8, 193–199

Walter, W. G., *The Living Brain*, Duckworth, 1953

Ward, J., 'Psychology', in *Encycl. Brit.* (9th Ed.), 1883, 20, 37–85

Warren, H. C., 'Some Unusual Visual After-effects', *Psychol. Rev.*, 1921, 28, 453–463

Warren, J. R., 'Birth Order and Social Behaviour', *Psychol. Bull.*, 1966, 65, 38–49

Weiskrantz, L., 'An Unusual Case of After-imagery Following Fixation of an "Imaginary" Visual Pattern', *Quart J. Exp. Psychol.*, 1950, 2, 170–175

Werner, H., *Comparative Psychology of Mental Development* (Rev. Ed.), Follett, New York, 1948

Werner, H. & Kaplan, B., *Symbol Formation: an Organismic-developmental Approach to Language and the Expression of Thought*, Wiley, New York, 1963

West, L. J., (A General Theory of Hallucinations and Dreams', in L. J. West (Ed.), *Hallucinations*, Grune & Stratton, New York, 1962

Wheeler, R. H., 'A Theory of Circuit Integration: a Criticism of the Centrally Aroused Process', *Amer. J. Psychol.*, 1928, 40, 525–541

Witkin, H. A., Lewis, H. B., Hertzman, M., Machover, K., Meissner, P. B. & Wapner, S. *Personality Through Perception*, Harper, New York, 1954

Wittkower, E., 'Further Studies in the Respiration of Psychotic Patients, *J. Ment. Sci.*, 1934, 80, 692–704

Wolpe, J., *Psychotherapy by Reciprocal Inhibition*, Stanford Univ. Press, 1958

Woodworth, R. S., *Experimental Psychology*, Macmillan, New York, 1938

Wyburn, G. M., Pickford, R. W. & Hirst, R. J., *Human Senses and Perception*, Oliver & Boyd, Edinburgh, 1964

Yarney, A. D. & Paivio, A., 'Further Evidence on the Effects of Word Abstractness and Meaningfulness in Paired-associate Learning', *Psychon. Sci.*, 1965, 2, 307–308

Zikmund, V., 'Oculomotor Activity during Visual Imagery of a Moving Stimulus Pattern', *Studia Psychologica*, 1966, 8, 254–274

Ziskind, E. & Augsburg, T., 'Hallucinations in Sensory Deprivation—Method or Madness', *Science*, 1962, 137, 992–993

Zlody, R. L., 'The Relationship Between Critical Flicker Frequency (CFF) and Several Intellectual Measures, *Amer. J. Psychol.*, 1965, 78, 596–602

Zubek, J. P., Welch, G. & Saunders, M. G., 'Electroencephalographic Changes During and After 14 Days of Perceptual Deprivation', *Science*, 1963, 139, 490–492

Zuckerman, M., 'Perceptual Isolation as a Stress Situation', *Arch. Gen. Psychiatr.*, 1964, 11, 255–276

Zuckerman, M., Albright, R. J., Marks, C. S. & Miller, G. L., 'Stress and Hallucinatory Effects of Perceptual Isolation and Confinement', *Psychol. Monogr.*, 1962, 76, Whole No. 549

Zuckerman, M. & Cohen, N., 'Sources of Reports of Visual and Auditory Sensations in Perceptual Isolation Experiments', *Psychol. Bull.*, 1964, 62, 1–20

Zuckerman, M. & Cohen, N., 'Is Suggestion the Source of Reported Visual Sensations in Perceptual Isolation?', *J. Abnorm. Soc. Psychol.*, 1964a, 68, 655–660

Zuckerman, M. & Haber, M. M., 'Need for Stimulation as a Source of Stress Response to Perceptual Isolation', *J. Abnorm. Psychol.*, 1965, 70, 371–377

NAME INDEX

Abbott, H. D., 30, 33, 37, 127, 128
Allport, G. W., 28, 30, 32, 33, 34, 40, 41, 127
Anderson, B., 81
Antonovitch, S., 72
Antrobus, John S., 44, 117
Antrobus, Judith S., 44
Ardis, J. A., 110
Armstrong, C. P., 88
Arnhoff, F. N., 108
Arnold, M. B., 58
As, A., 117
Augsburg, T., 103

Bain, A., 45
Bakan, P., 104, 105, 109
Barber, T. X., 19, 20
Barratt, P. E., 55, 65, 66, 136
Barron, F., 82, 106
Barry, H., 37
Barry, H., 37
Bartlett, F. C., 41, 62, 75, 132, 133, 137, 139, 143, 144
Bartlett, J. E. A., 120
Bennett-Clark, H. C., 33
Bergson, H., 139
Berry, W., 15
Betts, G. H., 45, 46, 47, 62, 67
Bexton, W. H., 101
Binet, A., 19, 29
Blake, W., 125
Bliss, E. L., 93, 104
Blyton, E., 125
Bocci, B., 17

Bond, I. K., 91
Boring, E. G., 13
Bousfield, W. A., 37
Brenman, M., 89
Brindley, G. S., 25
Brower, D., 79
Brown, J. L., 15, 21
Brown, B. B., xi, 71
Brownfield, C. A., 100
Bruner, J. S., x, 12

Camberari, J. D., 107
Campbell, F. W., 25
Carey, N., 79
Chowdhury, K. R., 73
Clark, L. D., 93, 104
Clark, L. V., 56
Cohen, L. D., 128
Cohen, N., 104, 105, 107, 108, 109
Coleridge, S., 125
Collier, R. M., 144
Cooley, C. H., 88
Costa, A. M., 111
Costello, C. G., 51, 55, 56, 66, 67
Coué, E., 10
Craik, K. J. W., 16, 17
Cruickshank, R. M., 21

Davis, F. C., 79
Day, R. H., 17
Deckert, G. H., 71
Diehl, C. F., 59, 61
Doob, L. W., 31, 37, 39, 40, 41
Downey, J., vi, 74

Downie, J. E., 18
Drever, J., 71
Drewes, H. W., 21, 67, 68, 83, 132
Dunlap, R., 146

Eichmeier, J., 111, 121
El Koussy, A. A. H., 54
Ellis, H., 121
England, N. C., 59, 61
Erickson, E. M., 19
Erickson, M. H., 19
Evans, C. R., 33
Everstine, L., 134
Eysenck, H. J., 52, 147

Fechner, G. T., ix
Feinbloom, W., 16
Féré, C., 19
Fernald, M. R., 62
Fisher, S., 114
Foulkes, D., 99, 106, 109, 112
Fox, C., 67, 81
Frederiksen, J. R., 133, 134
Freedman, S. J., 93, 98, 101, 102, 106, 107, 111, 112, 113
Freides, D., 33, 34
French, J. W., 54, 55, 133
Fromm, E., 123
Furst, B., 77

Galton, F., ix, 23, 36, 45, 50, 73, 82
Gastaut, H., 70
Gengerilli, J. A., 39
Gerard, R. W., 88
Ghiselin, B., 123, 125
Gibson, E. J., 134
Gibson, J. J., 134
Gill, M. M., 89
Goldberger, L., 105, 106, 109, 112, 114
Goldstein, K., 32
Goldstone, S., 114, 115
Goldthwait, C., 43
Golla, F. L., 63, 67, 71, 72
Gombrich, E. H., 142
Goodenough, D. R., 128
Gordon, R., xii, 50, 51, 52, 56, 92
Green, M. R., 123
Greenblatt, M., 101

Greenfield, P. M., 12
Gregory, R. L., 25
Griffitts, C. H., 45, 49, 52, 53, 73, 74, 97
Gruithuisen, F. P., 18
Grunebaum, H. V., 101

Haber, M. M., 109
Haber, R. B., 30, 33, 34, 36, 37
Haber, R. N., 30, 33, 34, 36, 37, 75
Hadamard, J., 27
Halpern, S., 89
Hanawalt, N. G., 22, 23
Harano, K., 10
Harman, W. W., 126
Harris, C. S., 75
Hartley, E. L., xi
Hayden, S. D., 27, 32, 37, 39
Hayden, S. P., 33, 34
Hebb, D. O., 5, 102, 120
Heermann, G., 61
Henle, F. G. J., 22
Heron, W., 5, 101
Hicks, G. D., 44
Hill, D. S., 76
Hirst, R. J., 1
Hodges, A. B., 38
Hofer, O., 111, 121
Höffding, H., 4
Holt, R. R., x, 105, 106, 109, 112, 114, 137
Homme, L. E., 130
Horowitz, M. J., 111, 120, 121, 122
Hovland, C. I., 87
Hume, D., 4, 5
Humphrey, G., 81
Hunter, I. M. L., 76
Hutchinson, H. C., 91
Hutton, E. L., 63, 67, 71
Hyman, R., 81

Imus, H, 15
Isherwood, C., 138

Jackson, C. W., 107
Jacobson, E., 58
Jaensch, E. R., 20, 29, 30, 31, 33, 37, 40, 42, 50
James, W., 8

SUBJECT INDEX